Top 100 Questions

Friends and Family Ask A Lawyer

Nelson P. Miller

Top 100 questions friends and family ask a lawyer.

Miller, Nelson P.

Published by:

Crown Management LLC – July 2014

1527 Pineridge Drive
Grand Haven, MI 49417
USA

ISBN: 978-0-9905553-4-6

For the friends and family members of lawyers.
Yes, your lawyer knows something useful.

Table of Contents

Introduction

People ask lawyers the darnedest questions.

The odd questions usually have that intuitive common sense that most of us possess (some more than others). The questions usually start from an unexpressed premise that most of us would readily accept, sort of like, "They can't do that, can they?!" We each have a sense of justice, fairness, equity, proportion, perspective, and the like. Some of us have that sense stronger, while others weaker. Yet we still share that common ground, or we would not much exist as a people. We each expect some property rights. We recognize what is *mine* and (less often) *yours*. We each expect a right to be left alone, at least that others would respect our bodily integrity ("Hands off, you lout!"), but even that others would respect our peace and privacy. The law recognizes and indeed relies on those intuitive rights. Our Founders called them *self-evident truths*, meaning natural rights and responsibilities that we can draw simply from our common existence.

Yet in any one instance, the law can look inconsistent with those fundamental truths and foundational rights. People pick up quickly on those places where law just might not be making the sense that it should. Those anomalies bother people—as the anomalies should. If people simply did what the law provides

1

without questioning its policy, rationale, equity, and justice, then, well, those unquestioning people wouldn't be American. They wouldn't be human. Our condition is constantly to examine and question the rules and routines by which we live, thirsting for their improvement, perhaps hoping to throw off their constraint even as we constantly rediscover the ageless wisdom of those constraints. So people should ask those odd questions when law seems not to make sense.

Lawyers are not always so good at answering the odd question. Lawyers have incredibly technical training. Oh my, the arcane things lawyers must learn in law school! When a lawyer hears the odd question of a family member or friend, the tendency is to think of the minutiae, the fine point, in the way of the detailed application that lawyers must do day to day. They go into lawyer mode, when the person asking the question needs a law teacher more than a lawyer. Yet lawyers are naturally good at teaching. They teach and advocate law to judges, opposing lawyers, clients, opposing parties, and other persons all day every day. They explain law orally on the telephone, in office meetings, in conferences, and in court, and in writing in correspondence, memoranda, pleadings, and briefs.

The challenge is to make sense of the question, to resolve its superficial anomaly based on the deeper purpose or finer balance that the law tries to achieve. The people are right: they need to understand law. Law must account for itself to the people. Lawyers need to explain and justify law to them. The people deserve answers. The first skill of a lawyer, whether the lawyer is just out of law school or has decades at the bar, is to make law understandable, pragmatic, rational, and effective, to justify it to those whom it affects. So here, for education, appreciation, and enjoyment of lawyers and the friends, family members, and clients of lawyers, are a top-100 questions that people ask lawyers.

100

Oh, How the Grass Grows

Question

The city just hung a warning on the doorknob of my home's front door saying it's time to mow my lawn. Can the city make me mow my lawn? It doesn't look that bad to me.

Answer

Get out the lawnmower.

You have the right sense that your ownership carries with it the privilege of getting to choose your property's use and maintenance. Property ownership is a bundle of legal rights. Primary among those rights is the right to exclude others from your land and then to do as you wish while you occupy your land alone. Generally, you may sit on your porch and drink iced tea on the hot summer days while your neighbors slave away over the meticulous appearance of their manicured lawns.

Yet none of your rights of ownership are absolute. Consider for example your right to exclude others from your land. While that right is extensive—you could bar your mother-in-law from your home and even have the police remove her, although no one would recommend it—the right is not absolute. Public necessity may require firefighters to enter or cross your land to put out a fire next door. Private necessity may require passersby to take momentary shelter in your garage from a severe thunderstorm. A salesperson would even have an implied right of entry to knock on your door unless you had a locked gate or a sign for no solicitation. The public official who hung the notice on your door was relying on that implied right of entry.

Just as your right of exclusive possession is not absolute, neither is your right to do as you wish with your land. Local zoning laws may place reasonable restrictions on land use. Building codes may place reasonable requirements on your construction. Health and safety laws may prohibit you from dangerous activities. The law of private nuisance would prohibit you from using your land in ways that interfere with neighbors' enjoyment of their own lands (think pig sty or garbage dump). The law of public nuisance would prohibit your uses from interfering with the health or safety of passersby (think shooting range).

Only when those restrictions are so severe that they effectively take your land from you do they run afoul of the U.S. Constitution's Fifth Amendment as a regulatory taking. The Fifth and Fourteenth Amendments prohibit local government from taking your property without just compensation. Making you mow your lawn is not a regulatory taking. You do have other constitutional protection. Under the Constitution's Fourteenth Amendment, local government must not deny you of life, liberty, or property without due process of law. Courts have interpreted the due-process clause to mean that general laws of this kind must be rationally related to a legitimate government end.

So, why do you think your local city council enacted this lawn-mowing ordinance? Sure, a council of conformists could have been making aesthetic judgments that the city would look better if everyone mowed their lawns. Yet basic property maintenance can

4

have broader effects. Rats, raccoons, snakes, and other animals that carry disease or present safety threats may lurk in unkempt lots. Think too of the broken-window syndrome that poorly maintained property can attract vandalism and crime.

So unless something else is going on, your neighbors are going to get to sit on their porches, drinking tea while watching you mow your lawn. As the sign on your doorknob likely informed you, if you don't mow your lawn, then the city probably will mow it for you. Then you'll get a bill for their services. If you don't like the city's demand, then talk to the city department about what low maintenance they would accept, or complain to your city councilperson. They may change the law. If your lawn is no worse than your neighbors, and they did not get the same notice, then find out why. Government officials should not be targeting, discriminating, or retaliating.

99

Rain, Rain, Go Away

Question

My basement flooded up through one of the floor drains in a downpour last night. A couple of other homeowners on my city block had the same problem. Who can I sue for the $5,000 the cleanup is costing me?

Answer

Not so fast. It all depends.

Generally, we have responsibility for our own property. If something happens to it that is no one's fault or is our own fault, then we bear that loss. Just because we suffer a property loss does not mean that we have a right to recover for it. While some government programs provide for disaster relief, the law generally requires you to show more than simply that you incurred a loss in order for you to have a remedy. The law's way of looking at it is that you need liability before damages.

If you have homeowner's insurance, then your insurance may cover that loss, depending on the coverage you purchased, applicable exclusions, and other details about the event. Insurance is contractual—a promise according to the terms of the policy. You need to read the policy. If the policy insures water damage due to backed up drains, then the insurer should pay, again assuming that no exclusions apply. Homeowner's insurance typically covers property damage due to accidents or other unintentional occurrences. You need not prove that anyone in particular is at fault in order for you to recover insurance. Indeed, you may even be at fault, and yet you would still likely have the coverage. On the other hand, insurers like to exclude flood and other water damage, particularly from backed-up drains. Go figure—fire damages might have been better for you than water damage.

So, get your homeowner's insurance policy if you have one, and read it and all exclusions and riders closely with the help of a lawyer if necessary. You probably would not need to sue anyone. Simply make the claim to the homeowner's insurer. If you bought the coverage, then the insurer will probably pay for the clean-up. If it does not pay when it should, then you can sue the homeowner's insurer. If the homeowner's insurer does pay, then it may sue someone else anyway to try to recover its payments. The law calls the insurer's action a right of *subrogation*, but you need not concern yourself with that right.

Let's say, though, that you don't have homeowner's insurance or that the insurance excludes water damage from backed-up drains. You may yet find some relief. Here, though, you or (more likely) a plumber or contractor whom you consult about preventing a recurrence need to determine why the drain backed up. If someone was at fault for causing your loss, then you may have a negligence action against them. Perhaps the builder of your house designed, supplied, or installed a defective drainage system lacking a required back-up valve or some other feature. Maybe your neighbors unreasonably diverted water off their property and onto your property in their drainage designs. If so, then their liability insurance may pay for your loss.

If you are thinking about suing the city, then think twice. The city may well have done something wrong in the design or maintenance of the storm drains. Try to find out. Speak to the city workers who come by checking storm drains. Contact the public-works department asking for answers. If no one will talk, then contact your council representative. If that fails, then consider making a Freedom of Information Act request to inspect all public records relating to the storm drains in your neighborhood and the storm that night. Maybe you will learn something about the city's storm drains in your neighborhood. If the city knew or should have known of a problem but did nothing about it, then you might possibly have a claim.

The city may well have liability insurance to cover your loss, or it may be part of a municipal league through which it shares accidental-loss costs with other cities. Whether or not you learn anything about the city's responsibility, consider asking the city to put you in touch with its claim representative. That representative may tell you all you need to know.

If you do find that the city was at fault but it won't pay up, then your challenge in suing the city may be governmental immunity. State law determines whether you have the right to sue state or local agencies. Some states grant broad governmental immunity, making it very hard to sue and win. Others grant little or no immunity, making winning much easier if you have a case involving the city's carelessness. Some states also have specific statutes having to do with damage from backed-up sewers and storm drains. At that point, you would likely need a lawyer to help you determine your rights.

In sum, your own insurance is your best bet. Beyond that, if the downpour was just a 100-year-flood kind of rain, an unpredictably freakish event, and no one was at fault, then you might be up the proverbial creek without a paddle. Yet for $5,000, it is worth checking out, isn't it?

98

Mending Fences

Question

Every year my neighbor's garden gets a little bigger, crossing onto my property. I was fine with it until he put a fence around it including the portion on my property. Now, I'm hopping mad. What can I do about my neighbor building a fence over part of my property?

Answer

Tell him to take it down, and if he doesn't, then call your lawyer.

Boundary disputes between neighbors are actually relatively common. Property lines get blurred. One neighbor thinks the line is here, while the other neighbor thinks the line is there. Most of the time, it makes no difference. As long as everyone is getting along, and both share use of the property, then the boundary doesn't much matter. Problems usually arise when one neighbor constructs a building, fence, deck, or driveway over what the other neighbor thought was the property line. Encroachments like these can reduce your property's effective size and value, and interfere with your private use and enjoyment.

At that point, you should have a surveyor confirm the correct boundary line. Old boundary markers are not necessarily reliable. A proper survey of the boundary line is what you need. Because your issue involves only a single boundary and no other parts of your property, you do not need a full survey. A boundary survey should be relatively inexpensive. You may or may not have had a survey done when you bought your property. Property legal descriptions, called *metes and bounds* descriptions, on your property deed recorded with the register of deeds determine the boundaries of your property. You need a surveyor to turn the legal description given in distances, angles, and compass directions into stakes in the ground marking your actual boundary line.

If you and your neighbor cannot agree about the fence after the surveyor establishes the correct boundary line, then call your lawyer. Avoid self-help. Taking down your neighbor's fence may lead to an argument, fight, and retribution. Keep the peace. You don't want to end up in jail on criminal assault charges. You could also end up liable in damages if your neighbor had the correct boundary after all, and you destroyed your neighbor's proper fence.

Generally, if you own the property, then you have the right to exclude others (including neighbors) from its use. If you don't want your neighbor gardening on your property, then you may certainly tell the neighbor not to do so, although then don't expect any future tomatoes or corn. If the neighbor continues gardening on your property, then you may build a fence to discourage the trespass. If the neighbor destroys the fence and continues to trespass, then you may file a civil action for a court order to prevent the trespass. If the neighbor violates the order, then call the police who may arrest the neighbor, or return to court for a contempt sanction. At some point, your neighbor should realize that you are serious. Property laws put the public police power behind your enforcement efforts.

10

Easements can complicate boundary issues. An easement is a non-owner's right to use an owner's property. Easements can be either express or implied. An express easement is one that a deed or other document or agreement define. Look at your deed, and you may see various easements. An implied easement is one that arises from the parties' actions and circumstance. Easements come in different types including for water, sewer, and other utility lines, hunting or fishing, or driveways or paths for access to other property. If you or the person who owned your property before you granted an easement to the owner of your neighbor's land, then you may be stuck with it. Consult your lawyer.

If on the other hand your neighbor has no express or implied easement, then you have one other concern to address. Property rights can also arise by what the law calls *adverse possession*. If your neighbor openly occupied your land without your consent for a long enough period, then the law of your state may recognize your neighbor's ownership. In some states, for instance, the period for adverse possession is 15 years. If you let the neighbor fence your land for that period, then you may lose title to that portion of your land.

So don't rest on your property rights. Use them, or lose them. And you know what they say: "Good fences make for good neighbors."

97

With a Will There's a Way

Question

My wife and I both have adult kids from prior marriages. I love my kids but am not so sure about hers, particularly her drug-addict son. How do I keep my suspect stepson from inheriting my hard-earned property?

Answer

Execute a last will and testament (a will). Now.

You may be right to be concerned. When someone dies with property but without a will, the property often passes according to laws that govern and *intestate estate*. How's that for a lawyer's phrase? It simply means an estate without a will. An estate is the legal device for handling your affairs after your death. The laws of intestacy tend to dispose of property the way that people generally would if they had thought of it. Most people would probably leave their property first to their spouse, if they had a spouse who survived them. So if you had no will, then under the laws of intestacy much of your property might go to your wife, which might be fine with you but only as long as she shared some with your kids and didn't let her suspect son get his hands on it.

12

Uh, right. Better not leave it to chance and a drug habit. No matter what your family arrangement, executing a will is the standard way of passing your property on in the manner that you desire. A will expresses your, well, *will* as to the disposition of your property. If you want your wealth to go to this person or that charity, then decide before you get injured or ill, become incompetent, and can no longer act. The time for a will is when you're healthy and can give responsible thought to it, not later when anything could happen.

Probate codes place some limits on your authority to direct the disposition of your property. Your estate must first pay your debts. Wouldn't that be nice if you could just have your debts disappear while your assets go to your family and friends?! It doesn't work that way. Unless you had credit-life insurance, car loans, credit card debts, even business debt if you have personal guarantees, all generally get paid before your heirs get what's left. Your estate would likely also have to pay personal taxes you owe, probate-court costs, probate or estate tax, and attorney's fees. Unless you have something left, no one gets anything. Many people die with no-asset estates, often leaving creditors unpaid.

Probate codes can also protect a surviving spouse. If, for instance, you willed all of your property to your adult kids and little or nothing to your wife, then she may well have the right to elect against your will. Your wife might take the share that the probate code provides for a spouse rather than the little or nothing you left her. Your adult kids would then get what was left.

Beyond paying your debts and ensuring that your spouse gets at least something, though, you have a great deal of liberty in choosing who gets your property after your death. You need only properly execute a valid will while you are competent and then ensure that your heirs can locate and probate your will after you're gone. For a valid will, state laws generally require appropriate language, competent disinterested witnesses, signatures, maybe notarizing, and a couple or few other specifics.

13

You want to give some real thought to your choice of personal representatives (executors or administrators), too, maybe both a primary and backup.

You have other ways to pass property on your death outside of a will. In some cases it can make sense to share title to certain forms of property now with the person whom you want to receive it, so that the property passes outside the will. Take care, though, because some transactions of this type can have hidden tax consequences. In the case of life insurance, you usually need only designate a beneficiary. In the case of certain accounts, perhaps a retirement or brokerage account, you may designate account beneficiaries. You may also form a trust, especially if estate taxes or the ability of the heir to manage the inheritance are concerns.

Sound confusing? It can be, but don't make it too much so. If you are well enough off to have property to share after your death, then simply be responsible about it. Have an estate plan. Get help from a lawyer whose practice includes estate planning. Don't let that suspect stepson take advantage of you, your wife, and your kids. And don't feel like you got yourself into a mess here. Your situation is actually pretty common. As you well know, things can get complicated in blended families. Clear communication of expectations and interests can help, especially around property and finances. Keep your house in order. Everyone will be better off for it, including your suspect stepson.

96

No Gutters but a Fresh Start

Question

I paid a guy a couple grand to put gutters on my house, but instead of him showing up to do the work, I got a postcard saying he's bankrupt and I can't do anything about it. What can I do to this scam artist to get my money back? I'm thinking a torch and pitchfork ought to be a good start.

Answer

Hold your horses, Lone Ranger.

If you gave a couple thousand dollars for gutters but did not get them, then you deserve your money back. Yet if the postcard was a correct notice that your gutter contractor has indeed filed for bankruptcy, then federal law protects the contractor under a bankruptcy stay. While you certainly may address the bankruptcy court to challenge the contractor's filing, you must not make other attempts to collect the debt while the stay remains in place. No torches and pitchforks, which of course would never be a good idea. You must also not telephone, email, write, or otherwise contact the contractor, or take other action other than through the bankruptcy court, attempting to collect the debt. If you do attempt to collect the debt outside the bankruptcy court, then the court may sanction you with fines and other penalties. The bankruptcy stay has the effect of a federal court order.

You may yet find some relief from the bankruptcy court. To file for bankruptcy means to petition the federal bankruptcy court for a discharge of debts. An order of discharge follows a process that may take several months or longer. The bankruptcy court does not grant every petition. Some filers do not follow through to the final order for discharge. Other filers do not qualify for discharge. Some specific debts do not qualify for discharge. If the contractor fails to obtain an order for discharge, then at the dismissal of the bankruptcy case you should be able to pursue the contractor once again for the debt (for instance, suing him in small-claims court). Depending on whether the contractor is an individual or company and plans to remain in business, the contractor may also be pursuing a type of bankruptcy in which creditors like you receive at least some payment from the contractor on your debt.

You are probably wondering about the justice of letting bankrupts take someone's money for nothing and then discharge the debt. The policy behind bankruptcy is to give deeply indebted individuals, companies, and even governments a fresh start. Whether by their own fault or not, debtors can simply reach a point of no return when they are unable to pay their debts. Rather than let them languish with crippling debt, bankruptcy gives them a chance to return to productivity, which can certainly be good for them but also good for society. Bankruptcy can hurt creditors in the short term. You may have lost your couple-thousand dollars. Yet bankruptcy can help creditors and others in the long term. The bankruptcies of General Motors and Detroit certainly hurt thousands of creditors, but those same creditors may have the opportunity to go right back to doing business with a healthier GM and Detroit, if they choose to do so.

Congress designed bankruptcy to protect innocent or foolish debtors, not scoundrels. One of the types of debt that do not qualify for discharge is a debt that the bankrupt incurred through the bankrupt's fraud. If your contractor was a scam artist who never intended to install gutters and was instead simply cheating you out of a couple-thousand dollars, then you may object in the bankruptcy court to the contractor's discharge, and the court should grant your objection, requiring the contractor to pay you back. Whether you actually got any money back would be another question. The proverbial wisdom is that you cannot get blood out of a turnip or water out of a stone. If the contractor is utterly financially and legally irresponsible, and for instance simply disappears to another state or nation, then best wishes in getting any money back.

So what do you do? Well, next time be sure that you are dealing with a reputable contractor, and maybe pay only part of the money up front. Creditors actually have many ways that they protect themselves against the risk of a debtor's insolvency, although that issue is for another story. As to your claim against this contractor, consider meeting promptly with a lawyer who represents creditors in bankruptcy proceedings to see if you have grounds to recover your money. The contractor may have treated other homeowners in the same way in a last-minute scheme just before a long-anticipated bankruptcy filing. If so, then that scheme may have been fraudulent, meaning that the contractor should not be able to discharge your debt. The other homeowners may also share in the cost of pursuing the contractor through bankruptcy.

So again, no torches and pitchforks, but check around. Look into it a little further with local suppliers and tradespersons who know the contractor. See if you can locate others whom the contractor treated in the same way. Get a committee of creditors together to contact and work with a lawyer promptly, before any of the bankruptcy court's deadlines pass. Your lawyer can examine the contractor in bankruptcy court, helping you to determine whether to proceed. And if not, then consider your this affair an education in how to identity and deal with poor financial risks. At least it was only a couple-thousand dollars.

95

Deadbeat Dads

Question

Hey, there's a billboard on my way to work saying, "Dead beat dads go to jail," showing an unhappy guy in an orange jumpsuit and handcuffs. What's up with that?!

Answer

The enormous decline of two-parent married households in America traps in generational poverty millions of single-parent families. Without adequate parenting and support, children in these families are many more times likely to commit crimes, suffer abuse and neglect, commit suicide, suffer physical and mental diseases, not graduate from high school, not get jobs, and not develop stable marital relationships in new families. For the first time, America has more unmarried households than married households. The median age of an American woman's first child is now lower than the median age of her first marriage. While these unstable demographics concentrate within certain minority populations, the trends apply across populations. These trends make child support a huge current public issue.

In response, public agencies and private nonprofit advocacy groups run advertising campaigns like the billboard you saw. Non-custodial parents are not always aware that child-support enforcement can include court contempt sanctions including jail. Jail provides a remarkable incentive for someone owing child support to earn, beg, or borrow that they would otherwise not have had. Also, custodial parents do not always know that their child has the right to the non-custodial parent's support. They also may not know that prosecutors and other public officials will often help them gain child support, particularly when the custodial parent receives public assistance.

If your concern is for the deadbeat mom or dad, then know that the law provides them with due process. The custodial parent must have a court case to obtain a child-support order. A child-support order depends on first establishing that the one from whom the custodial parent seeks support is in fact the child's other parent. Blood tests for paternity are common and usually quickly settle that matter. The amount of support must also bear a reasonable relationship to what the non-custodial parent can afford to pay out of earnings or other income. Courts ordinarily do not order support in amounts greater than the non-custodial parent can afford. The orders are often to the non-custodial parent's employer so that the custodial parent gets the support payment right out of the non-custodial parent's paycheck.

Support problems often arise, and support arrearages often accrue, when the non-custodial parent loses a job and, with it, the necessary income to pay the ordered support. The non-custodial parent should then immediately request the court to reduce the support amount. They often do not make that request, instead falling behind in support payments. Custodial parents or public officials acting on their behalf may then seek to collect the arrearage from bank accounts, tax refunds, and other income and assets of the non-custodial parent. If the non-custodial parent does not cooperate, then the court may order incarceration in jail as a contempt-of-court sanction.

Of course, you may wonder how someone in jail is possibly going to come up with the money to pay a support arrearage. Jail wages are not going to do it. Although jail is in no sense a perfect solution, courts may use brief periods of incarceration to test non-custodial parents' assertion that they have no assets. Sometimes, the money magically appears when jail threatens. In other cases, repeated periodic incarceration seems necessary to break the recalcitrant will of a non-custodial parent who could work and pay but just won't do it consistently. Unfortunately, custodial parents can abuse the system, and public officials and courts do not always get enforcement right.

If you know of someone who has a serious child-support issue, then encourage them to get good counsel from a lawyer skilled with support issues. Most of us want to support our kids. Some of us cannot always do so. The possibility of jail is simply to keep our intentions honest and efforts serious. Child-support enforcement by threats of jail should not be widely necessary. The fact that we see billboards for it comments aptly on our societal condition.

94

Doctors Versus Lawyers

Question

I just had my annual physical exam, and my doctor couldn't stop talking about the dastardly lawyers. Why do doctors dislike lawyers so much?

Answer

Malpractice. No one likes accountability.

Actually, doctors work closely with lawyers on many things. Lawyers help doctors form their practices as professional corporations. They help doctors lease their offices, govern their employees, contract with suppliers, comply with federal regulations, and protect their state licenses. Lawyers help doctors collect unpaid fees from their patients. They write wills for doctors and close on homes for doctors. Lawyers structure the public or private finances for the hospitals on which doctors depend. Doctors would be lost without lawyers, just as lawyers would be, well, dead or diseased without doctors.

What some doctors and medical associations object to are not really lawyers but the law, particularly malpractice law. When a motor-vehicle driver is careless and causes serious injury, the driver has liability (and usually insurance) to pay for the injury. The same liability holds true for homeowners, shop owners, manufacturers, and service providers — and doctors. Malpractice law is the same private law of care that applies to all of us. We simply call it *malpractice* (we also call it *professional negligence*) because doctors have special training against which we judge their conduct, rather than a general standard of reasonable care that we all follow.

The unique challenge that doctors face is that patients are often already sick when they see a doctor. Even without the doctor doing anything wrong, a sick patient can have a very bad outcome. In fact, even if the doctor does everything exactly right by the book, patients can still have very bad outcomes. Disease and death can be difficult things even when natural rather than human-caused. Some patients and their family members blame doctors, particularly when the doctor has not had the time, taken the time, or had or exercised the skill, to explain things to the patient and family in an appropriately sympathetic manner. Poor bedside manner is one reason why doctors face complaints. Malpractice lawyers spend a lot of time explaining to injured patients just what happened, when the doctor refused or was unable to give an explanation.

An even bigger challenge that doctors face is that some treatments carry serious risks of injuring the patient even when the doctor or other treatment providers do everything right. Surgical procedures, chemotherapy, radiation treatment, prescription drugs, and even physical therapy can all present risk of injury in themselves, never mind the underlying disease they are meant to address. The medical field calls treatment-caused injury *iatrogenic injury*, which remains a real concern for the medical field. The key for doctors is to inform their patients of those risks before the patient decides to accept the treatment.

Malpractice lawyers spend a lot of time explaining to injured patients that the injury was due to an unavoidable risk of the treatment, not anything that the doctor did wrong.

Studies have shown that the incidence of malpractice may be higher than the public generally thinks. The Institute of Medicine reported an estimate of up to 98,000 U.S. hospital deaths due to mistakes every year. The Office of Inspector General for Health and Human Services reported an estimate of 180,000 U.S. hospital deaths of Medicare patients alone due to bad care. A third report by a patient advocacy organization estimated 210,000 to 440,000 preventable U.S. hospital deaths every year, which would make it the third leading cause of death after heart disease and cancer. Studies also show that a small percentage of doctors is responsible for a large percentage of the malpractice cases. As is probably true in every trade or profession, a few incompetent practitioners make for a large number of bad outcomes. States require doctors to report malpractice judgments and settlements for review by licensing officials.

Despite the higher incidence of malpractice, the number of malpractice lawsuits may be lower than the public thinks. Studies suggest that a small fraction of those whom doctor malpractice injures actually sue. Harvard School of Public Health researchers found that most malpractice cases involve serious physical medical injury, not nuisance suits, and that most of the time the juries and insurance companies are getting it right, defeating the meritless claims while paying the meritorious claims. Statistics also show that doctors generally do better in malpractice trials than you or I would do as defendants in motor-vehicle-crash or other liability cases. People tend to like their doctor. Jurors respect doctors and their considerable training and expertise. Suing a doctor and winning is not easy, in part because of the high respect in which we hold doctors and in part because of the substantial resources that doctors and hospitals have to defend themselves against lawsuits by their patients.

Doctors also already enjoy substantial legal advantages in some states that other defendants do not share. Medical-malpractice laws in some states require that you tell a doctor that you intend to sue six months before you actually do so. Procedural rules require lawyers to file another doctor's affidavit confirming the malpractice, when they file the complaint. Evidence rules limit the experts who may testify against a doctor to other practicing doctors, making it hard for some patients to find qualified expert witnesses.

So on the whole, doctors have less reason to complain than they may suspect. Oh, and lawyers face the same malpractice liability as doctors. Next time your doctor complains, tell your doctor that if a lawyer screws up an important transaction for the doctor, then the doctor can sue. Turnaround is fair play.

93

Know Thy Friends

Question

My teenage kid had a bunch of friends in her car when police pulled her over for nothing. They found an open can of beer in the backseat that my kid didn't even know about, but they still charged her for it. What gives with that?

Answer

It could be some bad news here, friend.

You are thinking that because the beer was not hers, she shouldn't be charged as a minor in possession of alcohol. The trouble is that minor-in-possession is probably not the charge. More likely, your daughter's charge has to do with having an open intoxicant in the operated vehicle. Different crime. Sure, minors are not to possess alcohol. We don't want kids turning into drunks. They can do that later when they're adults! Yet a vehicle driver is not to allow open intoxicants in the operated vehicle. The open-intoxicant charge both keeps alcohol from tempting or distracting drivers and keeps drinking drivers from

26

passing the drink to a passenger when pulled over. Federal law encourages states to adopt open-intoxicant laws by diverting some federal road funding to alcohol education if the state does not comply. The open-intoxicant charge has nothing to do with minors in possession.

Your sense of unfairness probably also has to do with the fact that your daughter did not know of the open beer, which a friend had in the back seat. Your sense may be right. Crimes typically have a knowledge (lawyers call it *scienter*) requirement. If you didn't know of the wrong, then you're not guilty of it. Yet some crimes don't have a knowledge element. Whether you knew of it or not, you're guilty if it happened. Consult with a lawyer. Open-intoxicant laws vary from state to state. Some states have open-intoxicant charges in which the alcohol must actually be in the driver's possession, meaning known to the driver and within the driver's reach. Other states have open-intoxicant charges in which the drink need only be somewhere in the occupied part of the vehicle. Drinking and driving is even legal in a few states as long as the driver is not legally drunk.

Of course, the prosecutor may be able to prove that your daughter did know of the open beer in the back seat, especially if none of her friends will testify that it was their beer, not hers. The testimony of others in the vehicle may be critical. Your daughter may find that none are willing to admit possessing and opening the beer, especially if they too are minors and would face a minor-in-possession charge. Some states also prohibit passengers from having an open intoxicant in the vehicle, meaning that even an adult friend could face a charge. Presumably, the police interviewed your daughter's friends before pursuing the charge against your daughter. Because your daughter took the charge, you may not yet know the full story. Be sure that your daughter has a good lawyer with whom she can speak frankly about what happened. She may be too embarrassed to tell you.

Your daughter may still have a chance. You said that police pulled her over for nothing. Your daughter had the constitutional right to be free from unreasonable search and seizure. That means that police had to have some reason (call it an excuse if you want) to pull her over. If they had no reason, then the court might throw out the evidence that the police got by pulling her over, which would mean dismissing the charge. Yet police have a pretty easy time coming up with a reason. If your daughter's vehicle had a brake light out or she crossed the center line, failed to come to a complete stop, was going just a little too fast, or did not have on her seatbelt, then the police had cause to stop her, and the evidence is in. Her lawyer can help her evaluate.

Crimes involving alcohol and driving can have serious life consequences. In addition to any fine and even jail time, your daughter could lose her license, a job, and career opportunities. Even if she keeps her license, her vehicle-insurance rates may go way up. Yet even if your daughter is found guilty of the crime, don't give up hope. Many states have diversion programs especially for youthful first-time offenders. With a lawyer's help, she may be able to get the charge dismissed or conviction removed after completing terms of sentence. If not, then later she may still be able to expunge the conviction.

While your daughter should face appropriate consequences, be sure that she gets the legal help that she needs. One thing is certain, that she has learned to choose her friends with care.

92

Hoping I Never Need a Lawyer

Question

I saw in the newspaper that you are representing the paralyzed kid who fell from the grandstand, the drunken driver who drove off the bridge, and the executive whose new wife absconded to Brazil with his fortune. I hope I never have to visit your office! Why would I ever *want* to see a lawyer?

Answer

Maybe you should see a lawyer before crises hit.

You are absolutely right that lawyers are crisis managers. Personal injuries, criminal charges, family ruptures, and other crises can all happen without warning. No one wants to face those crises. When they happen, they can quickly have huge legal and financial consequences. Lawyers have the education, training, and skill to help you manage and make the best of those consequences. In the case of the child falling from the grandstand, a lawyer might help make an insurance recovery that would provide services to help with the child's care and rehabilitation. A lawyer might help the drunken driver into a substance-abuse treatment program to avoid a lengthy jail sentence, keep a limited license, keep a job, and feed a family. In the case of the jilted executive, a lawyer might help recover some of the funds or at least end the irretrievably broken marriage.

Yet while lawyers help clients recover from crises, they are also natural risk managers before crises happen. We all face risks. We could avoid much risk by not going to events, not driving, or not marrying (to use the above three examples), but then we would miss great opportunities. No risk, no reward. Life is risk management as much as or more than risk avoidance. Some of us manage risks better than others. Even the best of us can be pretty subjective about the risks that we face and how we handle them. All of us can benefit from having a lawyer's knowledge of risks. Lawyers know and manage risks because they know and manage consequences.

Take the examples you gave above. The executive whose new wife absconded with his fortune might have addressed some of those risks with a pre-nuptial agreement and related measures. Love can blind a person to things that a trusted advisor would see. Consulting a lawyer before the marriage might have helped the executive see the risks that the lawyer would see and then protect himself in advance against the consequences he now faces. Similarly, the family with the paralyzed child might with a lawyer's help have already established a health savings account, tax-favored educational account, gifts-to-minors trust account, or other special program or benefit for their child that would especially benefit the child in the event of injury. Even the drunken driver might have been in a better position to manage his crash with respect to motor-vehicle insurance, civil liability, employment rights, and other interests had he been consulting a lawyer in advance.

Lawyers are more than crisis managers. They are even more than risk managers. They are also inventive guides to improving your life circumstances. They help you preserve and protect assets, manage and reduce liability and debt, form and operate responsible businesses, recognize and protect intellectual property, manage and protect your personal estate, and manage your employment relationships. Some of the most successful individuals are those who identify trusted advisors, particularly lawyers but also financial managers, accountants, psychologists, ministers, and others who can advise them throughout life. Making a good life while avoiding major crises has a lot to do with discerning and following the sound path forward. Lawyers know those sound paths.

Think of it like an annual audit or examination. You wouldn't avoid seeing a doctor until you were sick, would you? Instead, you should see your doctor for periodic wellness checks to learn about your health and improve it before you face a health crisis. You wouldn't ignore your finances until you found that you were destitute, would you? Instead, you should balance your checkbook every month, keep a budget and balance sheet, and meet with your financial advisor and tax preparer every year to keep your finances in order. You wouldn't ignore your vehicle's maintenance, would you? Instead, you have a skilled mechanic change the oil and filters regularly, rotate tires, and check brakes before the vehicle's systems fail causing an accident. In the same way, meeting with a lawyer about insurance for personal liabilities or about a home sale, business plan, estate plan, and other legal rights, interests, and opportunities can keep your legal affairs in order while improving your peace of mind and prospects for prosperity.

So don't fear or avoid lawyers. Rather, get alongside a wise lawyer. Then listen, discern, and follow.

91

Paying in Pennies

Question

I am so mad at the utility company for charging me unjust fees that I figured I should do better than get mad and instead get even. I plan to get a load of pennies at the bank, dump them unrolled into a big bucket, and pay my bill at their office in thousands of pennies. What do you think of that?!

Answer

Although you may be thinking of not getting mad but instead getting even, sometimes it is better to neither get mad nor get even.

If you feel that you must protest a payment through some communication or action, then find a sounder, more civil, and more lawful way than pennies. Paying in pennies as an act of protest or retribution is not particularly original. It has also produced mixed results for those who attempted it and bad results for a few. Your purpose in doing so may be in part to embarrass and inconvenience your payment's recipient, even as you call attention to your protest of the payment. Chances are pretty good though that the person to whom you deliver or attempt to deliver the pennies will be neither embarrassed nor inconvenienced. The law just does not give you much help with this form of protest.

Those who pay in pennies believe and insist that pennies are valid currency that others must accept as payment. They are only half right. The federal Coinage Act does indeed provide in relevant part that "United States coins and currency … are legal tender for all debts, public charges, taxes, and dues." Pennies are good money. Yet the Coinage Act does not state that utilities and other businesses or local agencies must accept pennies (or any other particular money form) in payment. To the contrary, many businesses and agencies refuse various payment forms while welcoming or even requiring other forms. Some insist on cash, refusing credit cards and checks. Others refuse cash, insisting on credit cards, checks, or special tokens. Still others refuse to accept large bills over, say, $20, simply for security reasons.

To be "legal tender" as the statute states simply means that pennies are a valid offer of payment, not that the other must accept the offer. To *tender* payment is to provide it, to offer it. A shopkeeper or utility office need not accept the offer. Indeed, at times they may decide to accept no form of money, either because they are busy with other affairs such as inventorying or working with another customer or fixing the cash register. Refusing payment or limiting it to certain forms may not always be good business, but it is their right to conduct their affairs as they see best, whether for security, convenience, efficiency, or other reason. If the utility office does not want to deal with a bucket of pennies—and who would, which is exactly why you are thinking of tendering it—then it does not have to do so. The U.S. Federal Reserve would have to take your pennies, but no one else.

So what has happened when people have tried to pay in pennies? In one instance, prosecutors charged the payer with disorderly conduct when he strewed the pennies across the payment counter and onto the floor. In another instance, the payer incurred a late fee double the amount owed when the agency reasonably refused the raft of pennies for lack of available staff to handle them. In another instance, an agency was happy to receive payment in any form including pennies but reasonably insisted that the payer sit idly by while the agency verified accurate payment by counting all the pennies. In yet another instance, the payer filled the payment envelope with feces, sickening officials who opened it and subjecting the payer to civil liability for inflicting distress.

You see, the receiver retains control over their premises and business methods. Indeed, you generally find it both difficult and hazardous, not to mention generally unproductive and unwise, to spite anyone at any time over any matter. One sympathetic state legislator actually proposed legislation that would have required government agencies to accept payment in pennies, but the proposal went nowhere. Spite, vengeance, and retribution through inconvenient means just generally make bad policy. Instead, if you have a legitimate complaint with the utility charge, then consult a lawyer. Even if the issue is over just a few dollars, lawyers can file class actions that remedy and even punish wrongdoers for cheating customers out of small amounts. Consumer-protection, civil-rights, and other special laws may also provide for statutory damages, costs, and attorney fees to ensure that you have an opportunity to redress wrongs. So instead, consult a lawyer about the wrong the utility inflicted on you.

By the way, tax law may be to blame for pennies, anyway. Sales tax is largely why we continue to need pennies. Otherwise, sellers of goods and services could just charge round figures, and payers would pay in round bills.

34

90

The Constitution: Read or Alive?

Question

I hear all the time about judges who say we have a living Constitution pitted against other judges who say to read the Constitution as the Founders wrote it. Why can't Supreme Court justices just agree on the Constitution?

Answer

Glad to hear of your interest. The U.S. Constitution makes a good case for being the greatest secular document of all time. It certainly means a lot to Americans while also serving as a pattern for constitutions worldwide. The Constitution has led us through civil war, world wars, industrial and information revolutions, successive waves of immigration, huge demographic shifts, and all manner of other internal and external challenges. It somehow seems under so many different circumstances to strike the right balance between liberty and order, democratic governance and individual rights, change and tradition, and so many other competing, contradictory, or overlapping interests.

35

Under the Constitution's structure, Supreme Court justices do have the last say about the Constitution's meaning. The Supreme Court has exercised judicial review of the constitutionality of the actions of the legislative and executive branches of government since shortly after the nation adopted the Constitution. Yet Supreme Court justices have also disagreed or differed about how to read the Constitution for most of the nation's history. Supreme Court majorities decide cases. Justices in the minority publish their dissenting views, giving the Supreme Court a rich history of differing constitutional interpretations. In America, we do not hide our differences.

You are right that two dominant strains of interpretation have to do with those who believe we should read the Constitution in the historical meaning and context in which the Founders wrote it versus those who read the Constitution as an evolving document fitted to the norms and needs of the times. Within those two broad views, constitutional scholars see multiple other ways that justices read the Constitution. Those who emphasize the historical reading can be formalists, textualists, literalists, or originalists, for instance, while those who emphasize contemporary readings can be evolutionists, constructivists, or pragmatists. We actually have many ways to read the Constitution, each subtly or starkly different from the other, although reasonable to group in one or the other of the two major originalist-versus-evolutionist camps.

You are likely to have no success in getting nine Supreme Court justices to agree on a single theoretical method for interpreting the Constitution, although they actually do agree on many other things that in many cases are just as important or more important to the outcome. Judges everywhere including Supreme Court justices must respect and address the Constitution, statutes, and prior court decisions. Judges must rationalize and justify their decisions because they must maintain public confidence and the confidence of the other branches of government. Courts actually have little or no direct means of carrying out their judgments. They maintain no military or police force. To a large degree, their judgments must self-execute through the authority that we recognize within them. If instead, courts were all about ideology, then more of us would simply ignore them.

Most Supreme Court decisions do not divide along party lines. Many are unanimous or nearly so, and many more divide over mundane issues that the public would not recognize as ideological or controversial. Yet politics does contribute to divisions on the Supreme Court, particularly around the more-political or hot-button social issues. Presidents appoint Supreme Court justices with the Senate's advice and consent. As nearly everyone in America knows, those appointments tend to be highly political in nature. For example, as an Illinois senator, President Obama voted against consenting to the current Chief Justice John Roberts whom Senator Obama called unfit for the High Court. President Bush nominated Chief Justice Robert. Chief Justice John Roberts was then an esteemed member of the nation's second-highest court and will likely go down as a most-highly respected chief justice—even by the president. In part because presidents of different political parties nominate the justices, the justices tend to hold differing views about lots of things including interpretive methods.

Having multiple methods for reading and interpreting the Constitution is not a bad thing, by the way. The division or separation of powers, making it harder for any one person or faction to take sole control over the nation's course and governance, is the Constitution's central theme. Separation of powers usually refers to the three branches of government (legislative, executive, and judicial), to the federal and state systems, or even to the judge and jury. Wherever you see power, the Constitution tends to divide it. Yet separation of powers may also work as to the methods and ideologies by which judges read, interpret, and apply the Constitution. If judges all read the

Constitution the same way, then they might exclude important perspectives, insights, and interests of others.

So, do we have a living or historical Constitution? You and I may each have our preferences, but maybe it is better for all of us that we leave room to disagree.

89

Activist Judges

Question

From what I hear, some of these judges are just making it up as they go along, a bunch of activists. Where do judges find these things that they now call *rights* when a few years ago no one had heard of them?

Answer

The source of law is a very good and very important question. So is the motivation and role of judges.

Law actually has several widely respected sources, some of which might surprise you. Of course, judges find law in the texts that their oaths and offices bind them to follow. They must above all read and apply the Constitution. They must also apply the legislative enactments (statutes, codes, ordinances) before them. Judges, as you have heard, apply the law rather than make law, at least when it comes to cases controlled by statute. Judges also have a rich history of their own decisions to which they refer constantly. Lower courts must follow decisions of their higher courts, but even the higher courts respect and tend to follow their own prior decisions, even when the members of the higher court have changed. Judges value tradition.

Yet no doubt, judges have other influences outside of these traditional and obviously authoritative texts. One of the strongest influences on judges is other judges. We tend to adopt the views of those with whom we daily interact. Judging can be highly isolating. When all you see every day are the same appellate judges and law clerks, they tend to influence you, just as you influence them. Judges decide cases within communities of like-minded professionals whose opinions judges must value. Individual cases also influence judges. You might think you know what you think until you see something you have never seen before. Then you might think differently. So it also is with judges. Events of the day including social and political movements, and economic and technological change, also influence judges. Law is contextual. Law can look different in new contexts.

Decisions may seem at times like judges hold their finger up to see which way the political or social winds are blowing. Indeed, social norms influence judges. Decisions may also seem at times like judges have an ideology or agenda. Certainly, one's personal experiences and perspective, philosophical beliefs, and worldview or cognitive framework, also influence judging. Nevertheless, the convention that judges must justify their decisions within a legal rather than ideological, social, or philosophical framework to some degree forces judges to set aside these other considerations in favor of traditional legal considerations. When you disagree with a decision, you might think that a judicial opinion is lipstick on a pig, but lipstick can nonetheless change behavior (well, not on a pig but on a human).

Others can see when a judge is stretching the law to accommodate a non-legal decision. Judges are open to criticism, their opinions subject even to reversal. Most judges have at least some sensitivity to criticism and will attempt to avoid the worst of it when criticism is warranted. Most judges are also sensitive to reversal and will avoid making decisions that will not stand appellate review or the test of time. Many judges also face elections, which provides another kind of accountability. Those who do not face elections, like federal judges, still have reputations. They may not care about criticism from some quarters, but they will care about their reputation in other quarters.

The cases that judges decide also constrain the reach of judges. Judges may at times wish to accomplish certain things, whether economically, socially, or politically. They may feel that they know better than the legislature or executive that did or did not act in the way or at the time that the judge desired. Yet judges must wait for each particular case to bring before the judge the matter that the judge is to decide. Judges do not issue edicts. They decide cases. Enterprising lawyers and parties may find the cases to bring before activist judges to reach desired decisions, but decisions still require such cases. And even after a ground-breaking decision, a court depends on other branches of government, private parties, and even other courts to carry the decision forward.

So judges may indeed from time to time be activists, if by activism you mean deciding things that law does not then warrant. Judges do indeed make law from time to time, indeed often, even though we think instead of judges *applying* law made by legislatures. Law is not always evident. Judges decide cases of first impression, in effect making law where law gave no precedent. Still, because of all of the above limitations, we tend to think of the judicial branch of government as the least dangerous branch of government, not the most dangerous.

Judges get it wrong, in history even famously wrong, some of the time. The Supreme Court has upheld slavery, segregation, racial interment, and eugenics (forced sterilization of "imbeciles"), although the Court eventually reversed some of those decisions. We may feel at times like appellate courts are ignoring or

41

eliminating fundamental rights while attempting to alter the bedrock of society. Most generations have felt so over one issue or another. Yet when appellate courts perform at their worst, the other branches of government, the people, and history have eventually managed to overcome them.

Now there's a cheerful thought, eh? Judges have also given us shining examples of when to preserve the best of our commitments. While judges may sometimes look like activists, the nature of their roles and methods is fundamentally the opposite, to let tradition, practice, habit, and the wisdom of the ages be our guide.

88

My Keeper's Keeper

Question

I pay a friend through church to clean my house once a week because I have just had too much to do lately to keep up with housework. Now I'm hearing that I am supposed to treat my friend like an employee by withholding taxes. What's up with that?

Answer

Welcome to the nanny tax. Get out your accountant's pencil and your checkbook.

Actually, the federal government has no special tax for household employees. Rather, you are encountering the taxes that every employer must withhold and pay whenever an employee earns more than $1,900 per year (the figure for 2014). Those taxes apply to any employer including household employers of nannies, housekeepers, gardeners, and the like. Just because you employ a person at home, and just because your work is part-time employment of a friend, does not relieve you from the general obligations of employers. The IRS recognizes exceptions for paying your spouse, parent, or minor child, but in general, if you employ someone who earns more than $1,900 from you in one year, then you withhold and match taxes. If you pay your friend any more than about $36.50 per week for 52 weeks, then your friend would be earning more than the $1,900 limit at which you must withhold and match taxes.

The taxes about which you should be most concerned are the employee and employer portions of the Social Security and Medicare taxes, which together we call FICA. Employees must pay 6.2% of their income for Social Security taxes plus 1.45% of their income for Medicare taxes. Those amounts employers withhold from their employees' paychecks, meaning that you would reduce your payment to your friend by those amounts in order to remit those amounts to the IRS. Employers must then match those 6.2% and 1.45% amounts, meaning that you must match out of your own pocket the amount that you withheld for your friend and then submit the 15.3% total amount to the IRS.

Employers face other tax and reporting obligations in addition to withholding and matching FICA. Household employers do not have to withhold income taxes like other employers must. Yet household employers do have to pay federal and state unemployment taxes for employees earning more than $1,000 in any one quarter of the year. Unemployment taxes can be between about 2% and 10% of earned income depending on the state and the employer's claims rate. Household employers must also issue an IRS Form W-2 at the end of the year. You must also then file with your own tax return a Form 1040 Schedule H reflecting your household-employee tax payments.

You might wonder who would complain if you did not follow these tax laws. While both you and your friend would gain in the short term by not paying these taxes, your friend loses the Social Security credits and loses the value of your matching funds. Your friend is losing out. Employees tend to be the ones who complain. Household employers have faced some notorious losses of their own for not paying the nanny tax. A prominent lawyer whom President Clinton nominated to be U.S. Attorney General lost the post because of her failure to pay the nanny tax. You wouldn't want the nanny tax making a mess of your life just when something good was about to happen for you, would you? Lawyers, doctors, and other licensed professionals can face discipline affecting their ability to continue in practice over not paying the nanny tax. The IRS can add substantial penalties to overdue nanny taxes and can even pursue criminal charges. The problem is sufficiently serious that the IRS has offered an amnesty program to enable delinquent taxpayers to make up their nanny-tax payments.

As in so many things, the questions are not who would complain, whether you would get caught, and what would happen if you did get caught. Instead, give yourself the peace of mind. Follow the law because it is the law. While complying with payroll-tax requirements is quite technical, companies offer households nanny-tax services to relieve that burden. Many businesses, not just home employers, outsource their payroll services. Do the same to simplify your life while complying with the tax laws. You and your friend have a good thing going. Keep it a good thing. Do it right. If you owe the tax, then pay the tax, even if others tell you that you can get away with not doing so. Give to Caesar that which is Caesar's, or you will be giving Caesar power over your life that you would rather not face.

87

A Distinction with Big Differences

Question

I give a guy a few bucks to help me chop firewood that I sell as a sideline. I've always called him an independent contractor, but do I have to treat him as an employee?

Answer

Consider saying hello to your first employee.

Different state and federal laws define employees in different ways. Some laws use a traditional *control* test. If you control your acquaintance's activities while he works, particularly as to his time, tools, and methods, and whether you can hire, fire, and discipline him, then he is more likely an employee than an independent contractor. Other laws use an economic-reality test. If his work is integral to your business, then he is more likely an employee than an independent contractor. Still other laws (particularly tax laws) use an IRS 20-factor test that considers the above and several other sensible factors. Notice that the formalities such as whether you call him an employee or whether you issue an IRS Form 1099 (for contractors) or Form W-2 (for employees) at the end of the year make little or no difference. The substance of the relationship, not the formality, makes the difference.

You didn't tell me much, but it sounds like your acquaintance may be an employee rather than a contractor for most or all purposes. If he works with you when you decide to work, under your direction using your methods and tools, then he is more likely an employee than if he works when he wishes, doing the work as he wishes, using his own tools. If you decide whether he works at all, in the sense of hiring and firing him, and you decide whether he gets a pay raise or gets his pay docked, then he is more likely an employee than if he decides whether to work and receives the same whether he does a good or bad job. Because your business is chopping firewood, and he chops firewood rather than, say, changes the oil in your truck or repairs your equipment when it breaks, then his work is more likely integral to your business, making him an employee rather than independent contractor.

So why should you care? The distinction between employees and independent contractors can make a big difference in several areas. For example, federal and state minimum-wage and overtime-pay laws protect employees, not independent contractors. If your acquaintance is an employee, then you'd better hope that the few bucks that you pay him amounts to at least the minimum wage, or you'll be making up the difference. If he works more than 40 hours in a week, then you must also pay him time-and-a-half wages for overtime. For other examples, you must generally withhold and match FICA taxes, withhold state and federal income taxes, and pay unemployment taxes for employees, not independent contractors. You must also provide worker's compensation security for employees, not independent contractors. You face several other differences.

Treating employees as employees is especially important because of the potential for enforcement action. Your acquaintance may be fine with your informal arrangement now, but if you fire him or he gets injured, then things could change quickly. Worker's compensation officials, OSHA inspectors, unemployment-agency workers, and other officials may suddenly take a close interest in your arrangement, especially if your acquaintance claims the benefit of employment laws. The U.S. Department of Labor and the IRS have pursued joint enforcement initiatives against employers who misclassify employees as independent contractors. You should strive to comply with all laws but especially in the employment area where employers find frequent hazards of non-compliance.

So make an honest judgment about whether your acquaintance is an employee. If you do not want any employees but need his help, then tell him to go get his own worksite and equipment, and cut the wood on his time and his way, and then you buy it from him. If you don't mind having an employee but don't know how to comply with payroll and other requirements, then consult a lawyer or payroll service. In any case, keep it legal.

86

Wherefore Art Thou, Romeo?

Question

My cousin married a guy who turned out to have so many bizarre fetishes that no one could possibly live with him. They never really even managed to move in together. Can she just get an annulment and move on, or does she have to go through a divorce?

Answer

Close call. States limit the grounds for annulment, but your cousin just may have a chance.

An annulment declares a marriage null and void, as if the marriage was never a marriage. Courts grant annulments when one of the putative spouses shows that the putative marriage meets the statutory criteria for an annulment. Annulments differ from divorces in that divorces end marriages, while annulments determine that a lawful marriage never took place. Some religious organizations also grant or recognize annulments from the sacred (religious) rather than secular (law) standpoint. Your cousin should consult her religious advisors about those

49

requirements but would still need a court to grant an annulment for the law's purposes.

While states vary in their marriage, annulment, and divorce laws, states typically recognize annulments when the marriage wasn't a legal marriage. For example, to marry legally, you must not already be married. You cannot lawfully be married to two persons at once. Surprising as it seems, some people do marry a second spouse while still being married to a first spouse. In some cases, they believe the first spouse to have died when in fact the first spouse lives. In other cases, they believe that a court has ended the first marriage with a divorce judgment when in fact the court never entered that judgment. In still other cases, the bride or groom may know that they are still married to someone else but not understand the consequences (that the second marriage will not be a legal marriage) or do not care about those consequences. An annulment sets the public record straight, that the second marriage was never a marriage.

To marry legally, you must generally also be of a certain age (legal ages can be different state to state) and be mentally competent. States typically allow an annulment when one of the spouses is underage or incompetent. For other examples, while marriage laws vary state to state, marriage laws tend to require a marriage license, ceremony before an authorized individual (typically religious ordination or government official such as a judge or mayor), and consummation (sexual intimacy between the spouses). Spouses may be able to obtain a court annulment of the marriage if the license was not issued or was invalid, no ceremony took place or the ceremony was not before an authorized official, or the spouses did not consummate the marriage.

Annulments sometimes occur in connection with one of the spouse's fraud, particularly (but not solely) financial or immigration fraud. For example, a man seduces a woman into believing that he cares only for her when instead he cares not at all for her but instead for her money. They marry in a wonderful ceremony, but he disappears during the elaborate reception, managing in the process to steal her jewelry and drain certain of her bank accounts. With evident fraud and without consummation, the putative marriage warrants an annulment. For another example, a foreign national believes that marriage to an American citizen will qualify her for lawful resident status. She seduces a willing partner only to disappear with the marriage license and her partner's American name immediately after the ceremony. Again, with evident fraud and no consummation, the putative marriage may warrant an annulment.

So the mere fact that your cousin married a lout is not sufficient for an annulment. Yet if what you mean by never really managing to live together is that the marriage had no consummation, then annulment may be possible. Your cousin may also have other grounds. She should consult a lawyer who knows her state's law. And if her greater concern has to do with religious sensitivity, then she should consult her spiritual advisor. Next time, no surprises.

85

What Just Happened?

Question

My girlfriend and I have been living together a long time. Every once in a while, someone says something to one of us about common-law marriage. Are we married, and if so, then what difference does it make?

Answer

You may or may not be married at common law, depending on where you lived together, what you tell others about your relationship, and how long you have lived together. Maybe it is time the two of you clarified it?

Marriage is a matter of state law. Marriage typically requires a license, ceremony, and consummation between two consenting and competent unmarried adults. Many states once recognized common-law marriages in which the license and ceremony were unnecessary, and some states still do. While the state laws could vary, common-law marriage generally required that the two of you live together as husband and wife, consummating the relationship through sexual intimacy while holding yourself out to the public as if you were husband and wife, in a state recognizing common-law marriage.

Common-law marriages would thus typically arise between long-time live-in lovers who would soon tell others (the public) that they were married, when in fact they had no marriage license or ceremony. Common-law marriages did not always provide the certainty that traditional marriage with the license and ceremony provided. One party might think that the relationship was a marriage based on the parties' words and actions while the other did not. Both parties might also unintentionally satisfy the conditions for common-law marriage by, for instance, having a one-night stand at a hotel in a state recognizing common-law marriage after signing the hotel register as husband and wife.

Only a few states continue to recognize new common-law marriages. Around nine states clearly do recognize new common-law marriages, while a few more may for one purpose or another but not all purposes. As society's attitude toward unmarried cohabitation changed, many states gradually repealed their common-law marriage statutes and stopped recognizing new common-law marriages. Many states that abandoned their common-law marriage statutes nonetheless continue to recognize old common-law marriages, meaning ones that arose before the repeal of common-law-marriage statutes and abandonment of common-law marriage. States also continue to recognize common-law marriages formed lawfully in another state.

Policymakers have justified common-law marriage statutes as protective of the homemaker (non-income-earning) spouse. If when the relationship ends the income-earning party can have claimed all of the benefit of the putative marriage but have none of the post-relationship obligations of support, then the non-income-earning spouse may require the aid of the state and have suffered significant financial and legal oppression. Without marriage, the financially less-well-off party has little to no protection. You might remember the *palimony* case involving Hollywood star Lee Marvin whose live-in companion received nothing for her claim. Alimony (spousal support) may be available in a true divorce, but palimony (a non-legal term) is not generally available in the termination of a cohabitation relationship.

If after consulting a lawyer you learn that your girlfriend and you are not married, then to avoid confusion, fear, and oppression, and to increase confidence, care, and trust, then with lawyer help you and your girlfriend might enter into a cohabitation agreement. You can use such an agreement to identify whose property is whose, whose debts are whose, your current financial and other responsibilities within the relationship, and your future financial and other responsibilities if any in the event of the relationship's termination. Think of a cohabitation agreement as a prenuptial agreement where there is no marriage, only a live-in relationship. Often, it is best to work things out in advance. You just might find that your relationship improves. Or, you could make it easier and just get married, and then have the benefit of many dozens of federal and state marital laws.

84

Ambulance Chasers

Question

I just saw a great comedy show about a personal-injury lawyer who cares about nothing more than money. I don't see how you lawyers can stand yourselves. Aren't all lawyers just a bunch of sleazy ambulance chasers?

Answer

No, no lawyers are ambulance chasers. Yet exaggerated depictions of our profession sure make for good entertainment.

Ambulance chaser would mean a lawyer who follows an ambulance to an accident scene in order to solicit the injured person to sign a contingency-fee agreement as a new personal-injury client. That practice, if any lawyer did it, would violate conduct rules and could cost the lawyer's license. Lawyers must not pursue and speak with persons whom the lawyer knows to need representation, in order to represent the person for fees. Lawyers may advertise, and lawyers may talk to others about what they do (building word-of-mouth contacts), but lawyers may not seek out someone needing representation in order to solicit them. *Ambulance chaser* is a harshly negative term for a lawyer, not the kind of thing to call a lawyer whom you wish to befriend (sort of like calling a doctor a *quack*), although many lawyers would have a sense of humor over it.

Not only are lawyers not permitted to solicit, they must also not employ another person to do so for them. For instance, a lawyer must not have a legal assistant or secretary call up or go visit a potential client, unless of course that potential client has first contacted the lawyer. Once a prospective client reaches out to a lawyer, the lawyer may certainly respond in person. If an injured person calls a lawyer from the hospital room asking to meet, for instance, then the lawyer may certainly make a quick trip to the hospital to meet with the client. But lawyers must not simply make frequent hospital rounds hoping to meet an injured person in need of compensated representation, as depicted humorously in at least one Hollywood film. Personal-injury lawyers thus develop client relationships not by in-person contact but by standing or reputation, general advertising, referrals from former clients or others, and similar networks. The restriction on solicitation is in part because lawyers can be quite convincing in person and in part to protect individual privacy.

Only a small percentage of lawyers actually practice in the field of personal injury as plaintiff's lawyers. By far most lawyers have neither the skills nor inclination to practice in the personal-injury field. Personal-injury practice requires litigation skills, which many lawyers have but many other lawyers eschew. Some lawyers just do not like the contentiousness, fluidity, and unpredictability of the courtroom. They prefer the control and predictability of office-based transactional practice. Plaintiff's personal-injury lawyers must also be risk takers. They only get paid when they choose a case that results in a verdict and judgment or settlement. Personal-injury practice can be feast or famine. Personal-injury lawyers must also have a substantial degree of compassion for the seriously injured. Not everyone does. Many feel that the injured should just get on with it.

Personal-injury lawyers must above all be tireless advocates for the little guy or gal very much down on his or her luck. Few people are really in a position to care about the seriously injured and disabled. Their employers long ago gave up on them. Their doctors have generally done all that they can. Their neighbors can no longer depend on them. Their friends no longer find them to be any fun. Even their families are often just worn out caring for them. The injured clients themselves often feel utterly worthless, made so instantly after a horrible accident caused by the careless defendant. Those defendants have none of the injured plaintiff's disadvantages. They are usually happily productive and employed. They are routinely insured, meaning that they have at their defense the resources of well-funded insurers and skilled defense lawyers often from large law firms. The plaintiff's personal-injury lawyer, often a solo practitioner or from a small firm, has little more than the law and the truth, like David against Goliath.

These challenges are in large part why plaintiff's personal-injury work is one of the more lucrative practice fields for lawyers who are skilled, courageous, and well-connected enough to make a consistent go of it. With risk goes reward. While you shouldn't expect to find the clichéd flashy trial lawyer of television and film, and certainly not a literal ambulance chaser, you will find among personal-injury lawyers a wide range of characters perfectly at ease with who they are and very effective at getting others, like judges, jurors, insurance companies, defense lawyers, and defendants, to see things their way. Surely don't think of them as sleaze. They are often gifted with gravitas, sometimes highly humorous, and always fascinating. They are also critical protectors of and resources for the injured poor. Imagine yourself in the place of a suddenly seriously injured and disabled person, and you will gain a whole new appreciation for the plaintiff's personal-injury lawyer.

83

Lawyer Presidents

Question

You lawyers seem to have a lot of power, from the top on down. Why are so many American presidents also lawyers?

Answer

Twenty-five of the nation's 44 presidents have been lawyers — well over one half. Lawyer presidents include Thomas Jefferson, James Madison, John Quincy Adams, Abraham Lincoln, Woodrow Wilson, Bill Clinton, and Barack Obama. President Obama is the second Harvard Law School graduate to become president after Rutherford B. Hayes. Two other presidents, Theodore Roosevelt and Harry Truman, were law school dropouts, which is to say that they each began law school and received some law training without earning a law degree.

Lawyers make effective political leaders in part because of their training in logic, reasoning, policy, and articulating and evaluating arguments. Their training in legal research, precise and persuasive writing, public speaking, and advocacy contributes to their technical and affective skills as political leaders. Law practice also helps lawyers develop wide and effective networks of many other leaders having diverse and substantial interests and resources. Abraham Lincoln is an example whose law practice first serving individuals and later serving national corporate interests developed for him both a sterling reputation and substantial network of contacts for later political office.

The fact that some presidents are lawyers does not guarantee that they will be effective presidents. The U.S. House of Representatives impeached one lawyer-president Bill Clinton for perjury and obstruction of justice over the sex scandal with his aid. The Senate acquitted him. The House would have impeached another lawyer-president Richard Nixon not too long ago had he not resigned after the House Judiciary Committee voted out the articles of impeachment. The other U.S. president that the House impeached, Andrew Johnson (also acquitted in the Senate), was not a lawyer.

The tradition of lawyer leaders stretches well back beyond the nation's founding. The leaders of ancient Rome were often military generals, but one of the most famous, Cicero, was by training and experience what we would today call a lawyer. Of course, Cicero's eloquence in argument, particularly that Rome should once again be a republic free from tyrannical leadership, lost him his head—literally. One of his critics removed his severed head from its public display in order to open its mouth and stick pins in the tongue that had argued so brilliantly against tyranny. Sometimes, the effective advocacy of lawyers makes them too much of a threat as national leaders.

Lawyers make frequent and effective leaders in other areas outside of politics. For example, lawyers are sometimes company CEOs. Lawyers lead around one out of ten of the nation's largest 500 companies. Burger King, American Express, Cisco, Home Depot, Viacom, Nokia, Toys R Us, and Pfizer have all recently had lawyer CEOs. Those lawyer CEOs tend to credit their legal training with making them effective predictors of business success and failure, effective risk managers, and creative problem solvers. Interestingly, the opposite may not be true, that business leaders would make frequent political leaders. Business majors have not been frequent American presidents. George W. Bush was the first American president to hold an M.B.A. degree.

You should probably not be concerned about lawyers being too powerful. First, clients need and want their lawyers to be powerful and persuasive. You would want a well-respected and well-connected lawyer advocate if you needed one to protect something important to you like your life, liberty, and property. Second, the kind of power that lawyers generally possess is only the power of advocacy. Rather than having the power to grant you your wish, lawyers instead have the power to appeal to judges, administrators, governors, and others for your wishes. Third, citizens govern America by laws, not persons, in theory at least. The kind of power that lawyers typically possess is delegated and constrained power, not personal and unlimited power. Even lawyer presidents have only delegated and limited power, again in theory at least, Bill Clinton's impeachment and Richard Nixon's near-impeachment and actual resignation proving the point.

So don't worry about lawyer presidents. Instead, turn your concern toward that for which they advocate. Evaluate their arguments. Keep them accountable to that which you believe is best for the country.

82

Politics and Lawyers

Question

Lawyers must be the most political of all professionals. When politics so divide Americans, how can you stand to be around so many lawyers of the opposite party? You must have a very thick political skin.

Answer

Not really. No problem.

While lawyers certainly know politics, and many were undergraduate political-science majors, within their profession lawyers are instead seldom political. New law students sometimes expect law school to be highly political. Most law schools are not political because the methods of lawyers are not political. One of the first things that new law students discover is that the kind of evaluation and reasoning in which lawyers engage is not political opinion. Lawyers do not generally have political agendas. While lawyers are just as adept as anyone else at discerning the political leanings of others including other lawyers, nonetheless within their profession relationships and roles lawyers are largely apolitical (without politics). Certainly, their clients have agendas, but clients do not retain lawyers to accomplish political agendas so much as to accomplish personal and business agendas.

Everyone has an opinion. Studies of the ways that non-lawyers argue show that they often argue from the standpoint of who they are rather than what logic, policies, or evidence support their arguments. Non-lawyers often argue as if others should accept their argument because of who the arguer is, perhaps even because of how passionately the arguer feels about their argument. To lawyers, the identity of the advocate, or even the advocate's passion, is no reason to accept an argument. Lawyers evaluate arguments based on internal logic, external policies, supporting evidence, and similarly objective and rational bases. Just because the advocate shouts louder or pounds the table or weeps in passion over the argument does not make the argument any stronger or weaker.

So, then, just because someone happens to be a Democrat or Republican or Independent, or just because a position happens to be a part of the platform of a certain political party, really makes little or no difference to lawyers. When lawyers get together in the courthouse or at other locations, their small talk is usually not about politics. Their small talk is often about developments in the law and its practice, about the challenges they face and successes they see in their cases and causes. Don't get me wrong. Lawyers can certainly be as passionate about issues as non-lawyers. Yet when lawyers feel passionately about something, their feeling is often based on the obvious logic of their premise and illogic of the premise's opponents. If their opponent has the greater logic, policy, and evidence, then a lawyer had better be ready to find another case, cause, or argument. Lawyers cannot afford, and their clients cannot afford, to let their politics attempt to dictate outcomes.

The other thing that lawyers know about politics is to stay away from it when working with other lawyers, even (and indeed especially) opposing lawyers. Lawyers must relate effectively to and communicate effectively with their lawyer opponents. At times, they must even work well jointly with their lawyer opponents, such as when scheduling depositions, drafting a joint pretrial order, or documenting a settlement. Politics does not help with professional relationships and communication. You know the adage that family reunions have only two off-limit subjects for conversation: politics and religion. Lawyers will often go to great pains not to alienate their opposing counsel on whom they may depend for a scheduling convenience, procedural courtesy, substantive compromise, or (ultimately) settlement.

Some lawyers and law firms lobby for and otherwise represent political organizations. In those few instances, a lawyer's politics can certainly matter to the client, and the client's politics can matter to the lawyer. One may also find some broad patterns, for instance, that lawyers representing unions may tend to be of one political party while lawyers representing management of the other party, or that prosecutors would tend to be of one party while defenders of the other party, although one would find plenty of exceptions to those patterns. Otherwise, lawyers generally find it better not to know the politics of one's clients, professional adversaries, or professional allies when work needs to get done that has nothing to do with politics.

81

Surprisingly Not Humorless

Question

The other day I happened to have two lawyers out on my boat with some other friends. I was surprised to have such a good time with them. Aren't most lawyers humorless?

Answer

You're joking, right?!

Lawyers probably do have the reputation of being boring, which when you think about it is actually hard to understand. Lawyers deal day to day with everything that is social and human. They deal with the triumph and tragedy, the sublime and ridiculous, the making and breaking — everything. You really want to know how the world works, what goes on in your community, how the rich and poor, and the famous and infamous, alike live and die, love and hate, and think and don't think? Then just talk to a lawyer. The experience of a new lawyer joining the profession is almost precisely like getting to look behind the curtain to see how the wizard *really* works. Lawyers learn things like why spouses really divorce, why surgeons and airline pilots really make fatal mistakes, and why rich patriarchs sometimes leave everything they own to their cats.

Of course, lawyers must keep their clients' confidences, so don't expect any lawyer to regale you with the community's scuttlebutt. What lawyers are able to do though in social conversation is to reflect an insight into how we all think and act. The moment you think that people would *never* do *that*, a lawyer can confirm for you that indeed they do precisely *that*, and then give you the odd and eccentric reasons that people give for it. A lawyer's mind holds a record of the acts and consequences of the broadest range of human merit from the worst of sinners (truly, triple ax murderers) to the best of saints (true heroes). The lawyer's experience is not simply the experience of a reader of the daily newspaper but rather of actually getting to know, represent, study, perhaps cross-examine those whose actions make the news. Lawyers are more than able to entertain and fascinate.

Yet you asked about humor specifically, not just fascination with all things human. Lawyers can definitely be funny. Humor is not the gift of everyone, and the same we can say about lawyers. But lawyers certainly have the human fodder for humor, and many are quite good at making use of that fodder. The events with which lawyers generally deal are not in themselves funny. The weight of lawyers' dealings must be why you assumed that lawyers are generally humorless. A homicide charge, a wrongful-death action, a sexual assault—nothing funny about those events. Even a bond issue, a partnership agreement, a supply contract—nothing particularly funny there. Lawyers though must make sense of each of those events, whether positive or negative, or productive or destructive.

And lawyers know better than most that humor or something approaching humor, like wit, comicality, or absurdity, often makes the most sense of the mundane, weighty, or tragic event. Humor is very close to pathos. Joy is very close to pain. The traditional makeup for the funniest clown is to wear a big painted frown. The richer the humor, the greater its tinge of sorrow.

Clients facing the greatest loss, whether for instance the sudden death of a loved one or a bitter divorce, will sometimes simultaneously weep and laugh, seeing in the weight of their tragedy the absurdity of their human predicament and thus an odd lightening joy. Lawyers find themselves saying, "I mean, it shouldn't be funny, but ...," and then retelling the most amazing tales of human perseverance and perversity, funny in themselves.

One lawyer represented a widow and her children in the sudden and violent wrongful-death of her very smart and successful husband. Right in the midst of the protracted, technical, complex, and expensive litigation placing millions in damages at stake, the widow suddenly started dating and then got engaged to a muscled, bronzed, foreign-national man half her age. He even had a name that was roughly a foreign equivalent to *Romeo*, which the lawyer began using to refer to him outside the widow's presence. The lawyer was furious with his client the widow for accepting Romeo's pursuits, as the lawyer saw the huge damages case for her considerable grief disappearing out the window with the budding joyous relationship. Where was all of her heartfelt grief? But years later, long after the case had settled, the lawyer could do nothing but think again of the very sad but very human story — and somehow laugh.

No, for the most part, lawyers are anything but humorless. The lives that lawyers encounter, guide, and counsel are far too rich in pain, sorrow, joy, and absurdity to do anything other.

80

No Good Deed Goes Unpunished

Question

My husband and I let a single mother and her child come stay with us for what was supposed to be two or three days. Days turned into weeks, then weeks into months. When after three months she flatly refused to leave, she said simply, "So sue me." The police won't do anything without a court order, and they cautioned me against changing the locks. Do I really have to sue the ingrate to get her out of my own house?

Answer

Welcome to landlord/tenant court.

Police will act to keep the peace. If your family's safety were at risk due to violence or threats, then you would have had their help. On the other hand, police are not in the practice of settling civil disputes, meaning disputes over rights and property that do not involve breaches of the peace. If police took sides in every civil dispute, then they would far too often be creating or destroying interests inconsistent with the parties' actual rights. Police cannot in a few minutes of time when responding to a call, accurately resolve who gets to do, control, or keep what, when, and where. About the best that police can do in situations like yours is to keep the peace while maintaining the status quo.

If you had called the police after the first few days to remove the mother and child as disinvited guests from your home, then the police may well have done so. Trespass laws would have backed you up. Yet at some point, a guest can start to look more like a tenant. While landlord-tenant laws vary from state to state and even city to city, they tend to define a *tenant* as a person who occupies a specific part of the premises for at least 30 days paying or promising to pay rent. You are not running an apartment house. It sounds like you neither asked for nor received any rent and had neither a written nor even an oral lease. You let the mother and her child into your home out of the goodness of your heart. But they have now been in your home for more than 30 days, perhaps supplying some household services even if not rent. Whether the law defines them as tenants or not, now that the police have refused to remove them, you are probably stuck with going to landlord-tenant court.

Just to be clear, changing the status quo to reflect your actual rights is up to you, not the police, and through the courts, not by self-help. Here are the problems with your idea of changing the locks. First, doing so may lead to a breach of the peace. You, your tenant, and the locksmith may have a physical struggle or fight in the process of changing locks, or you may find your guest breaking in a door or window to access your home even if just to remove any property belonging to the guest. Second, you must dispose in some fair manner of your guest's property in the course of changing the locks. You cannot simply leave it locked inside your home, depriving your guest of clothing and other personal effects. If you put it on the curb, then others may steal it, or weather may destroy it. Third, for these reasons your state's landlord-tenant laws probably prohibit both changing the locks and putting your guest's personal property on the curb. Check your state's laws, but you might end up paying your guest damages or even punitive damages for either action.

Police will enforce court orders, though. When you obtain an order for eviction, the police will come to your house and maintain the peace while you remove your guest's property and change your locks. So your question is really how to get that court order. Again, landlord-tenant laws vary, but they typically require that you serve your guest with a written notice to quit, wait a statutory period that can vary from as little as three days to as long as 30 days, and then file your eviction action in landlord-tenant court. While notices to quit slow eviction, they serve the important social purpose of enabling tenants to find another home. You especially will not appreciate further delay, but your best course may be to act swiftly serving a proper notice to quit so that your delay is not working in your guests favor. Consult a lawyer who knows the landlord-tenant laws of your jurisdiction. Small consolation, but you may be able to recover some of your costs in going to court.

While self-help is generally unwise, and going to court looks may well be necessary, you may have one other option. You pretty plainly have a highly irresponsible guest who also happens to be a parent. This situation cannot be good for the child. You may find a child-protective-services official in your community who already knows of this parent's situation or should know. That official may be able to arrange other suitable housing for this mother and child. You may also find other nonprofit or religious organizations who have the social services to help. My guess is that you have already tried those things without success. You may just need the law. The law is there for you, but be sure that you do it right. Get a local lawyer's help with landlord-tenant court.

79

Hang Them by Their Thumbs

Question

My elderly parents just fell victim to yet another mail swindle. First, it was a sweepstakes that they were always just about to win, somehow connected with magazine subscriptions that they didn't need, and advertised by a kindly old celebrity whom only their generation would remember. This time, it was a prince from a foreign land who just needed a few thousand of their dollars in order to share his fortune with them. What can we do about these scam artists other than string them up by their thumbs?!

Answer

Although I like your thumbs idea, defense, not offense, is the best strategy when anyone, whether elderly, mentally disabled, or otherwise, loses the ability to recognize and avoid fraud or otherwise manage their money.

Unfortunately, the elderly and infirm make obvious targets for swindlers, so obvious that anyone having a family or other close relationship with such a person should be on the lookout to protect them. You simply cannot catch and punish all of the scammers before they get to your parents. Scammers are too numerous and too good at avoiding detection. Notice the snail-mail offers that they send. The return address is routinely a Post Office box, not a fixed address. Even if you found an address for the scam artist, you would likely find no identifiable person or entity at that address. Scam artists are usually way too smart to enable their detection. And as soon as you put one out of business, three more would take that one's place.

Instead, you and your parents have at least a couple of straight-forward protective measures. Any competent adult who wishes to may execute a power of attorney to let a better money manager handle their finances for them or at least help them with those finances. Elderly parents often execute a financial power of attorney in favor of their most-trusted and nearby adult child. A power of attorney would not keep your parents from wasting their money on a scam because they would still have money control, but a power of attorney could keep you more-closely involved so as to diminish their temptations. You would become their first line of defense against swindlers.

When an elderly or otherwise infirm person becomes incompetent, losing the ability to manage their own money, a probate or family court can approve a conservatorship in favor of a trustworthy adult child or other conservator. The incompetent person would then have no control over their own finances. At that point, the conservator becomes more than a first line of defense. With no money within their control, the incompetent person protected by a conservatorship would no longer be a fraud target at all. So the best way to protect your parents is to surround them with love, meaning in this instance to try to get them to see their need for your assistance beginning with a financial power of attorney in which you would share financial management and then perhaps letting you take over entirely or establishing a conservatorship if necessary.

Some offers, perhaps like your magazine-subscription example, may actually be legal, depending on the accuracy of the

71

accompanying disclosures. If law permits a sweepstakes, and someone somewhere someday actually does win according to the advertised odds and offers, and the participant even gets a few magazine subscriptions along the way, well, what they do with their money is largely their business. You can certainly speak with your parents about it, encouraging them to make better use of their time and money. But sad as it sounds, I have heard the companies offering those sweepstakes argue that they are actually doing the elderly a favor by keeping them engaged and making them feel wanted. Don't let your parents depend for attention on a smiling old celebrity enticing them into wasting their money on sweepstakes and magazines.

Other offers though, like your prince-from-a-foreign-land example, are outright schemes, scams, swindles, and frauds. A fraud is a false or misleading statement inducing your parents to rely to their detriment. Your parents could sue the prince for return of their money if they could ever find him, which they won't because there is no prince, just a hidden scam artist. If it's too good to be true, then it isn't true. Instead, before it happens again, get your parents to show you any offer they receive that they think might be legitimate and is attracting them. Of course, you'll recognize immediately that it is scam. But show your parents how to call your state's fraud hotline (often a division of the state attorney general's office) with a description of the offer. The good folks there will have heard of just about everything. You can also contact the Better Business Bureau. If it makes them or you feel any better, then you can also report snail-mail scam offers to the Postmaster General whose investigators may confirm a mail-fraud crime.

Yet remember, their interest in scams may suggest isolation. Help them find new activities and friends to keep them healthily engaged in real things. Let someone else worry about catching the scam artists and hanging them by their thumbs.

78

What's Ours Is Ours

Question

My husband just ran off with his sailboat and the man who crews it for him. No matter. Good riddance. My question is about how we will divide our property. His name is on everything. Am I up a creek without a paddle?

Answer

Probably not. Your ship may have just come in.

State laws determine how spouses will divide property in the event of a divorce. Whose name is on what may in the end make little difference, depending on your state's law. Most states follow the common law's *equitable distribution* system in which the parties to a divorce first identify their property as either marital property or separate property. Marital property is generally anything that either party earns or acquires during the marriage other than gifts and inheritances. Whose name is on the account, deed, or title is not the deciding factor. Separate property is anything that either party owned before the marriage plus those things acquired during the marriage by gift or inheritance. Separate property can become marital property if commingled with marital property.

In the divorce, parties then each keep their separate property but divide the marital property equitably. The parties to a divorce may of course agree on the property division. If he wants the boat and you want the home, then go for it. If you disagree, though, then the court will make the division for you. Courts generally total up the value of the marital property and then evaluate the division based on the percentage of the value that each party should receive. While an even split of the property (50/50) may be a good starting point, the court may give either one of you more of the property to account for things like your ability or inability to support yourself after divorce and your relative fault in bringing about the divorce. An *equitable* division means one that is fairest to both parties.

A few states follow slightly different community-property rules. In a community-property state, the parties first divide their property into community property and separate property. The definition of community property can be like that of marital property in a common law state except that community-property states can give more weight to things like the formalities with which the parties treated the property. If the parties agreed that the property was to remain separate, documenting that agreement by names on accounts, deeds, or titles, then it may not be community property. While determining what is and is not community or marital property can be difficult, common law states tend to classify more property as marital than community property states classify as community. Community-property states then tend to divide community property equally (50/50) between the parties, while each party keeps his or her own separate property.

Just a few other notes about your marital or community property. That part of a pension or retirement account earned during the marriage is marital property or can be community property, even when in the name of just one spouse and earned solely by that spouse. The same would be true of a business operated by one spouse, that appreciation in the business's value during the marriage would be marital and could be community property. The policy is that while one spouse earns the income, accumulates the pension or retirement account, or builds the business, the other spouse is doing something just as valuable to the marriage such as keeping house, raising kids, or simply caring for the breadwinner. Oh, and debts get treated under the same rules and divided accordingly.

If you and your sailor husband have substantial assets, then you need a lawyer's help to determine their division in divorce. While the percentage division (50/50, 60/40, etc.) is certainly important, you may also face other important issues like whether you want to stay or should stay in the marital residence. You may love your home, but if in order to keep the home you have to sacrifice other assets, particularly cash assets necessary for your support, then maybe it is time to downsize. Effective counsel can help you with these difficult decisions. You are not up a creek without a paddle. Sailorman may be the one whose ship is out to sea.

77

Not Knowing All

Question

I was reading the state journal yesterday about that appellate court that made such a crazy ruling on that municipal tax issue. It sounds like the appellate judges had no idea what they were doing. What do you think about whether they were wrong or right?

Answer

Send me the article or link, and then let's talk about it.

The nation has 50 different state court systems, each with one or even two levels of appellate courts. Many mid-level appellate courts divide themselves up into districts or panels, each deciding their own assigned appeals. One mid-level appellate court may have multiple different districts and panels constantly publishing new decisions. The federal court system operates similarly, dividing its mid-level appellate court up into circuits and panels, each deciding their own assigned appeals. Appellate courts decide thousands of cases every day, publishing hundreds of opinions. Their decisions fill bookshelves, volume after thick volume, taking up whole floors of libraries.

Lawyers use many ways of keeping up to date on the law but could not possibly keep up with all developments in all areas. Lawyers follow minute-by-minute social-media feeds and read daily e-journals with case summaries, weekly legal news, and monthly law magazines. They belong to listservs and attend periodic conferences. Most of all, though, they are constantly researching the law and interacting with other judges and lawyers who are researching the law. Lawyers know what they need to know. They just may not know what you know from reading a certain newspaper.

Lawyers are very good though at quickly finding out what they need to know to talk intelligently with you or to counsel or advise you about new law. A couple of minutes of electronic research will get a lawyer not just the news report but the actual case opinion. A lawyer can also readily locate within a few minutes and read the other authority that the new case opinion cites. Within a few minutes, the lawyer will have a pretty sound picture of the latest law development. News reports are not always accurate pictures of case holdings. Lawyers are especially good at placing new law developments in their proper context. A news reporter may believe a case to be unusual or ground-breaking when it is not. Lawyers tend to know better, especially when the new case is in their own field.

The number and breadth of law fields is part of the problem that lawyers have in keeping up with case and other law developments. Law practice includes literally dozens of distinct fields. Immigration lawyers know immigration law but not necessarily bankruptcy. Bankruptcy lawyers know bankruptcy but not necessarily employment law. Employment lawyers know employment law but not necessarily agricultural law. Agriculture lawyers know their field but not necessarily the field of environmental lawyers who don't necessarily know the field of tax lawyers who don't necessarily know the field of military lawyers who.... You get the picture.

New law is also constantly developing. Legislatures enact codes and statutes, sometimes including sweeping legislation that codifies and perhaps federalizes prior state case law. Administrative agencies promulgate thousands of new regulations. Applying that legislation and those regulations to the myriad of circumstances that arise day to day raises thousands of new issues requiring new case interpretation. The law will never have any end of case law. The situation is not one of eventually getting all law defined correctly to the point of running out of cases and questions. As society, technology, and other things change, laws will change, and cases will teach us more about how those laws work in any one situation.

Talk to your lawyer acquaintances about any new case decision you see. If the new case is in that lawyer's practice area, then chances are good that the lawyer will know the case. If the case is from a different field, then the lawyer will have the skill to help you learn more about the decision. Give a lawyer a chance, and the lawyer will find you sound answers about the latest law.

76

In It for the Money

Question

I saw that new lawyer in town at the country club yesterday. She pulled her top-class Mercedes Benz right up next to mine in the parking lot. You lawyers must all be alike, driving your fancy cars out to your country clubs and second homes. Tell me, you're all in it for the money, right?

Answer

Far from it, my rich friend. You'll find both rich lawyers and poor lawyers, and everything in between.

Lawyers can make substantial incomes, depending on the practice area, practice model, geographic area, skill, reputation, and experience, among other factors. Census Bureau and Department of Labor figures show that lawyers comprise as much as eight percent of the top one percent of household income earners. Lawyers on average earn significantly less than physicians and chief executives of larger corporations but significantly more than most trades and other professions. Median lawyer annual income is currently just over $90,000, although many lawyers earn a multiple of that amount. Lawyers probably represent around 10% of U.S. millionaires. If your goal in business is to make a lot of money, then doing so may well be possible. The same is true for lawyers. Lawyers who want to earn and save lots of money stand a reasonable chance of doing so.

Lawyers earn higher income in a variety of ways. Some lawyers earn higher incomes by taking few very large matters, whether those matters involve development deals, wrongful-death cases, estate plans, white-collar crimes, or other subjects in which both the stakes and the returns are high. As in any field, with risk can come reward. Those lawyers must have premier skills. Clients will entrust their highest-value matters to those premier lawyers as if they were the LeBron James, Phil Mickelson, or Kobe Bryant of the lawyer world. Wouldn't you hire one of those lawyers if your life, freedom, or entire fortune depended on it? The point remains that very few lawyers qualify for this premier-practice model. Statistically speaking, basketball and golf are extremely difficult sports in which to earn a fortune, unless of course you are born as Tim Duncan or Ernie Els (both major sports stars).

Other lawyers earn higher incomes through higher volumes, again whether in worker's compensation, personal injury, estate planning, Social Security disability, criminal defense, municipal law, corporate law, finance law, or other practice. Lawyers managing a volume practice must ordinarily have premier marketing, interpersonal, and systems-management skills. To have a volume practice, you need volume, generally requiring effective marketing and interpersonal skills. Also, lawyers must handle every matter competently. Lawyers cannot handle many matters competently without having in place trained and supervised associates and staff employing perfected processes and systems. In volume practices, only the partner or partners at the management top of the practice earn the higher incomes. Associates at the labor bottom of the practice earn moderate incomes. You'll see the partners, not the associates, at your country club. And these practices usually have many more poor (relatively) associates than rich (relatively) partners.

Most lawyers, though, occupy the middle of the income spectrum. In that broad middle, you will find lawyers in all practice fields and settings. Lawyers in plaintiffs' personal injury or in corporate practice tend to earn more than lawyers in most other fields, although one finds plenty of exceptions. Lawyers in larger firms tend to earn somewhat more than lawyers in smaller firms, although again one finds plenty of exceptions. Lawyers in metropolitan areas tend to earn more than lawyers in rural areas, although even here one finds exceptions. Although it would be hard to find proof for this assertion, lawyers are probably on the whole better financial managers than non-lawyers given a lawyer's professional duties and training. So while lawyers at their $90,000+ median make a significant though not exorbitant amount more than the approximate $50,000 median for other wage earners, they may also be managing those finances more effectively.

Then of course, some lawyers occupy the bottom of the income spectrum. Lawyers have very low unemployment, just under 2% according to the U.S. Bureau of Labor Statistics. Yet some lawyers are underemployed for various reasons including changes in practice areas, demographic shifts, technology shifts, or just having started or just finishing a law career. They would like to earn more income but aren't presently able, just as you would find in any other trade or profession. Other lawyers occupy traditionally low-income practice niches like indigent defense and legal aid. Some of those lawyers do so happily as a long-term career commitment, finding other deeper rewards in the work. Other of those lawyers do so less happily and more temporarily as a short-term career transition.

So, my rich friend, you'd see more of the average- and low-income lawyers if you spent less time at the country club. Oh, and by the way, are you driving your Mercedes up to your cottage on the big lake this weekend?

81

75

My Unemployment

Question

A while after I got laid off at the mill, my buddy offered me a job doing rough carpentry with his team again, something that I'd done before. I told him that I'd start when my unemployment ran out in a few more weeks. I figure I'd earned it. Nothing wrong with that, eh?

Answer

Well, yes, something likely *is* wrong with that, and it could include criminal fraud. Think about taking your buddy's job fast while stopping any more unemployment. And see a lawyer.

The federal and state governments coordinate in providing for unemployment compensation. In broad outline, the federal government charges employers a federal unemployment tax (yes, an additional tax on top of corporate income tax, matching FICA employment taxes, and other taxes) based on their payroll. The federal government reduces the unemployment tax if the employer is also paying a state unemployment tax as is usually the case, essentially giving the employer credit for unemployment taxes paid to the state. The federal government then backstops state unemployment programs during periods of high unemployment when those state programs become underfunded, as in the last deep recession.

Unemployment claims matter to employers. Employers pay more in combined state/federal unemployment taxes when they have more claims for unemployment. Employers pay less in unemployment taxes when they have fewer unemployment claims, creating an additional incentive to manage their workforce well. State programs essentially maintain bookkeeping accounts showing where an employer stands relative to the unemployment taxes paid in and the unemployment claims paid out. When an employer manages its workforce well, with few layoffs or other terminations qualifying for unemployment, the employer's unemployment tax can go down substantially. When an employer has frequent qualifying job terminations, the employer's unemployment tax can go up substantially. In short, both the state and the employer have financial interests in paying only valid claims.

The policy of state unemployment programs is to provide modest needed short-term financial assistance to the newly unemployed who are employable, to reduce the impact of job termination while smoothing their swift transition back into the workforce. Unemployment programs are not paid vacations. Employees do not "earn" "their" unemployment in the nature of accumulating personal leave days. While state laws differ in some respects, unemployment programs generally require workers to show that they worked long enough to qualify for benefits, that their termination was not due to their own willful disregard of the employer's interests, that they remain able to work, and that they are actively seeking but unable to find work. Layoffs are common grounds for unemployment claims.

The vast majority of unemployment claimants are honest. A few, though, either misunderstand what it means to seek work actively or outright misrepresent their work efforts, offers, and opportunities. Unemployment payments are so modest (typically only a couple or few hundred dollars representing only a fraction of the earned paycheck) that they leave a substantial incentive for the unemployed to return to work. Yet some studies, trends, and accounts do indicate or suggest that the receipt of unemployment benefits can discourage some workers from taking available jobs. Not every such instance involves a claimant's fraud. A claimant may have legitimate questions over whether any one available job is truly a job for which the claimant qualifies, for instance. The relatively small size of the benefit and fact that the benefit lasts only for a limited period (typically six months but extended recently and variable state to state) tend to provide strong incentives to return to work rather than attempt to rely on benefits for which the claimant does not qualify.

In your case, though, you used to work for the friend who is offering you a return to that job, which you plan to take as soon as your unemployment benefits run out. Those circumstances clearly indicate that you have employment available. You should take extreme care not to misrepresent to the unemployment agency your ability to find a job. Agencies and other government officials responsible for catching and discouraging fraud often have the resources to pursue claimants who have received unemployment benefits unlawfully. Those claimants may have to pay back the benefits received, with added penalties, costs, and interest. They could also face criminal fraud charges. You should consult a lawyer promptly about any such concerns.

Unfortunately, disreputable employers can also attempt to game the system. When a claimant worker applies for unemployment benefits, employers typically have the opportunity to object to the application. Some employers may object when they have no grounds to do so or when the employee can prove, on a disputed claim, the necessary circumstances for qualifying for benefits. Yet some claimants do not understand or are reluctant to respond to the employer's objection. In other words, employers may attempt to take undue advantage of a terminated employee's confusion or reluctance to pursue benefits over the employer's objection. Don't let an employer push you around, but by all means, don't misrepresent your opportunities to take benefits for which you do not qualify.

74

Your Protected Class, Please

Question

I never get any of the breaks at work. My supervisor is always passing me over for promotions, pay raises, and bonuses, and then dinging me on evaluations. No one else there gets treated like me. It's discrimination, plain and simple. I can sue for that, right?

Answer

Close, but not quite.

Federal and state laws make certain forms of discrimination unlawful. Employers who violate those laws may have to hire, reinstate, or promote the claimant employees who prove such discrimination, grant them pay raises and bonuses, and even pay those claimants other damages including in some cases mental and emotional distress. Yet those anti-discrimination laws require more than mere discrimination for the employer's action to be unlawful. For the employer's discrimination to be unlawful, and for the employee to have a remedy, the employer must have based the discrimination on one or more specific protected categories, characteristics, or classes.

Think of it this way. In its non-legal sense, to *discriminate* simply means to distinguish. Employers distinguish among employees all the time for many different reasons. Most of those reasons are lawful. Employers generally have the authority to do as they wish within their management interests with regard to whom to hire, promote, compensate, demote, and terminate. For instance, if an employer wishes to hire or promote one employee over another because the first employee has more education, skill, or experience, then the law would generally allow the employer to do so, even though the employer is *discriminating* based on education, skill, and experience. The law does not attempt to run an employer's business for it. Courts are not particularly well equipped to do so and would not be particularly effective in doing so.

Instead, federal and state anti-discrimination laws constrain employer decisions only around certain protected classes, categories, and characteristics. Employees without legal training often think that to discriminate alone is unlawful, when instead to discriminate *because of* a protected class, category, or characteristic is unlawful. The public nonetheless does recognize several of the classes that federal law protects including race, religion, sex, age, and disability. Federal law also prohibits discrimination in employment based on military service and genetics. While varying from state to state, state laws can recognize additional categories, prohibiting discrimination based on things like height, weight, marital or family status, and sexual orientation or identity. Federal and state civil-rights laws may also prohibit discrimination against one or more of these protected classes not only in employment but in education, housing, public services, public accommodations, and other activities.

Notice the large number of protected classes, categories, and characteristics — and we're probably not done yet. Some locales have made it unlawful for employers to discriminate against the *unemployed* for instance, creating another protected class. Federal and state laws also protect *whistleblowers* in certain cases. In practice, all of us are members of multiple protected classes. Any employee could thus in theory claim discrimination over any adverse employer, provided that they had evidence that the employer acted based on one or more of their protected characteristics. Employees are sometimes able to do so based on overt expressions of bias like the acting supervisor's racial or sexual slur connected with the adverse action. Other times, employees may attempt to use evidence that an employer practice, while not overtly based on a protected class, nonetheless has a disparate impact on a protected class, for instance when a workforce of some size somehow ends up entirely of one race or sex despite a diverse pool of employment candidates.

If you think that your employer is discriminating against you based on a protected characteristic or class, then report that action promptly to your employer. Federal and state laws prohibit retaliation for those reports. If your employer does not promptly address your concerns to your satisfaction, then promptly file a complaint with state and federal equal-employment-opportunity officials. You may need to exhaust these administrative remedies to preserve all of your rights. Above all, promptly seek a lawyer's counsel. The laws are complex, and time requirements can be tight. Just be prepared to identify your protected class. Employers must be able to manage their workforces. They do not always get it right. The law though prohibits only invidious discrimination, the sort of wrong that has to do with bias against your class.

73

Harass or Harass?

Question

My boss at work is always harassing me. I heard about a worker winning a million-dollar lawsuit for harassment. I just want him to leave me alone and let me do my work. What does it take to get him to stop?

Answer

If your sex has something to do with it, then one complaint to human-resources should do the trick. Otherwise, you might think about another job.

Federal and state employment-rights laws protect workers against sexual harassment and sexually hostile work environments. Those protections extend also to race and other protected classes. Yet harassment alone is not necessarily actionable unless the harassment is due to your sex, race, or other protected characteristic, or you can tie it to some other protection such as retaliation for whistleblowing or your exercise of other protected rights. A moody boss who unfairly yells, blames, and picks on workers, is generally bad management and bad for morale and business. But if your supervisor's harassment has only to do with trying to get you to do your job, then his conduct is unlikely to be unlawful even if uncivil, unfair, and unwise.

Blatant sexual-discrimination cases, the ones about which you read leading to substantial verdicts, typically involve a supervisor propositioning a subordinate for sexual favors and, when the subordinate refuses, firing or demoting the subordinate. Beyond the repugnant job-for-sex discrimination cases, sex discrimination can take a sexual-harassment form in which supervisors or co-workers subject a worker to sexual slurs, jokes, and other speech and conduct even including sexual touching. While a single slur or incident might not be unlawfully harassing, when the incidents are sufficiently severe and pervasive as to change the quality of the work environment, making it intolerable for the reasonable worker, then the law gives the worker a remedy.

Sexual-harassment cases tend to turn on the quantity and quality of the sexual conduct. While harassment that does not relate to sex, such as general yelling and bullying, might not alone be actionable, when tied to other conduct that does have sexual conduct, it can increase the workplace's hostility. When as in your case the conduct involves a supervisor directing harassment at a subordinate, rather than co-workers harassing one another, the hostility can increase. The nature of the workplace can be important. Sexual banter in some workplaces such as in certain trades may have less of an impact than in other workplaces such as professional settings. If the worker welcomes the conduct, perhaps even engaging in the sexual banter or consenting to sexual requests, then the employer may have a defense to that worker's claim, although how welcome the conduct really is, and what truly constitutes consent rather than coercion, raise difficult factual issues.

Human-resource managers within companies are typically very sensitive to these concerns. They know the legal risks to ignoring sexual-harassment complaints. Worker remedies can include reinstatement to the job and damages for any lost wages and benefits, and mental and emotional distress. Harm to an employer's reputation and the morale of its workforce add to sexual harassment's costs. You should be notifying the appropriate official within your workplace under its sexual-harassment policy, which you should find in your employee handbook. Give your employer a chance to fix this problem before you consider suing. Notice to the employer is a key part of any such claim. Consult a lawyer about these rights, especially if your employer has no policy in place, does not take prompt and effective remedial action, or (worse) retaliates against you for reporting your concern.

If your boss is just mean rather than a sexual harasser, and your employer won't do anything about it, then finding another job may be your best option. Tell the employer, though. The employer may not tolerate too many good workers leaving for other jobs. Firing the coach on a losing team can be better than firing the players.

72

Liar, Liar, Pants on Fire

Question

You must have seen the comedy film *Liar Liar* about the lawyer who makes a complete mess of his law practice when he suddenly can no longer lie. How many of you lawyers are pathological liars?

Answer

None.

Most pathological liars can't get into law school, no less get out and pass the character-and-fitness requirements for licensure. Certainly, the world holds its fair share of pathological liars. To get into law school, though, an applicant must show the character and fitness to practice law. Law schools tend not to admit applicants with criminal convictions, civil judgments, bad credit, school discipline, and other history indicating untruthful character. Law schools maintain honor codes to ensure that students reflect truthful character throughout the curriculum (including supervised law practice), dismissing students who lie or cheat. State bars then complete thorough investigations of candidate character, sending suspect candidates before character-and-fitness panels and refusing to license dishonest candidates.

If any pathological liar did manage to get a law degree and license, then they would quickly get caught and lose their license. Once in practice, lawyers must comply with conduct rules that specifically prohibit lawyers from all manner of lies and misrepresentations. Under those rules, lawyers must not present false evidence. If they know their client or witness to be lying, then they must not present that testimony and must disavow it if already given. They must not knowingly make false assertions of fact and must correct assertions that they later learn to be false in a pending proceeding. Lawyers must not misrepresent the law and, when their opponent misses favorable controlling law, must inform the court of law working against them. Outside of court, lawyers must not misrepresent their role, representation, or purpose when speaking with others. Even when advertising, lawyers must not mislead the public, make unsubstantiated comparisons, or create unjustified expectations.

Lawyers take these conduct rules seriously. Anyone may complain to state bodies regulating lawyers. Those bodies have professional staff who review and investigate complaints, and charge dishonest lawyers in disciplinary proceedings. Those proceedings may result in private or public censure, license suspension, and license revocation, along with costs and restitution. State bars publish discipline results so that every other lawyer and judge knows not to deal with the suspended or disbarred lawyer. Unauthorized practice of law statutes then prohibit those lawyers from practicing in the jurisdiction. Other jurisdictions will learn of the discipline and refuse to license the lawyer. Lawyers can lose everything by lying.

Courts have their own rules under which judges may further penalize lawyers and their law firms when the lawyer lies in court proceedings. The penalties can directly affect pending cases, resulting in case judgments or dismissals. Courts can also impose monetary sanctions in small and very large amounts, depending on the effect of the lie, and can refer lawyers for discipline. When a lawyer's dishonesty affects a client adversely, the client may sue in fraud or malpractice for the resulting damages. Lawyers may also be subject to criminal charges under federal and state laws against suborning perjury, obstructing justice, or mail and wire fraud. The stakes are extremely high for lawyers when the question involves honesty and dishonesty. Every lawyer takes truthfulness seriously.

Comedy though can have a ring of truth. In this instance that ring probably has to do with the nature of disputes. Many stories, indeed most of them, have two sides. One side may feel as if the other side, including the other side's lawyer, is lying, when in fact evidence supports multiple different versions of an event from multiple different perspectives. When parties dispute facts or interests, each side may be half right, the truth resting somewhere between them. Lawyers help the parties explore those facts and interests. Lawyers are usually very skilled in recognizing when the truth rests closer to the other side's version than the version believed or at least related by their own client. Often, the skill of a lawyer rests in the lawyer's ability to help his or her own client see the merits of the other side's contention, even as the lawyer gets the other side to see the merits of the contentions of the lawyer's own client. None of those skills mean that the lawyer is lying. Indeed, the contrary would be true, that the lawyer's skill depends entirely on the trust that others must have in the lawyer's honesty.

Lawyers are human. Lawyers can practice honestly and diligently for years, doing great good even for decades, and then suffer some mental illness, or succumb to some extraordinary temptation, or simply have some character breakdown resulting in dishonesty and disbarment. Lying can happen. Yet the pathological or routine liar would not be able to license as a lawyer and would not survive long at all in law practice. Liar lawyers make for good comedy precisely because the parody is *not* truthful.

71

May I Get a Word in, Please?

Question

You should have heard two lawyers arguing on television the other day. They were practically yelling at each other, and I'm sure neither heard a word that the other said. You lawyers take the cake when it comes to argument. How can you get a word in with one another?

Answer

Viewers expect television to entertain. Don't generalize everything you see on television.

Sure, some lawyers foster the persona of being belligerent. Some clients expect a fighter and will pay for it. Yet belligerent argument seldom gets a lawyer anywhere other than to impress a naïve client. The kind of argument that lawyers make best is logical argument, argument that persuades by its content rather than by the passion with which the lawyer imparts it. Logical argument begins with identifying the issue that the circumstances raise. Lawyers are masters at crystalizing and characterizing the disputed issue. Logical argument then identifies the authority, experience, evidence, and policy that informs the issue, just the sort of marshalling of data for which lawyers train. Logical argument then employs various forms of reasoning to arrive at justified conclusions.

While yellers may impress television audiences and the naïve client, lawyers who argue logically impress judges and (in most cases) juries. Judges have the same training as lawyers. Judges see right through belligerence. Indeed, judges do not permit the kind of uncivil argument that you sometimes see portrayed in entertainment. When lawyers start to employ theatrics with judges, judges will sometimes admonish them to "save it for the jury." While jurors generally lack legal training, cross-sections of the community comprise juries. Juries may have some members whom impassioned but unreasoning argument impress, but juries tend also to have logical members. They may be accountants, dentists, nurses, or schoolteachers rather than lawyers, but they will nonetheless have the education, experience, and temperament to evaluate arguments logically.

Lawyers actually do make keen listeners, too. Lawyers are especially effective in catching the meaning, phrasing, interest, motivation, confidence, and credibility of clients, opposing parties, opposing counsel, witnesses, and others. Watch a lawyer take a deposition, for instance, and you will notice how the lawyer picks up on the witness's slightest hesitation, odd phrase, or reluctance to answer. Lawyers seldom interrupt a witness at deposition, instead coaxing the witness to say more and more until the witness has said more than the witness wanted to say to make the point that the witness had hoped to make but for the lawyer's keen ear and open-ended questioning. Watch a lawyer as the opposing counsel makes an argument at a hearing, and you will notice how the lawyer anticipates, hears, and records every key statement, and then addresses those statements one by one in rebuttal argument. Prevailing is not a matter of drowning out the other side but hearing out the other side, whose arguments the lawyer must contradict or balance.

The work of lawyers is also not solely or even primarily win-or-lose advocacy. Lawyers are principally problem solvers, especially in transactional work in which lawyers bring parties together around agreements that serve multiple interests. Yet even in litigation, lawyers are in essence working toward resolutions that most often serve multiple interests rather than solely the interests of their own clients. As much as lawyers compete and advocate especially in the litigation arena, the vast majority of litigated matters resolve by compromise and settlement. Argument in that context is not a bludgeon by which to beat down an opponent into submission. Argument instead communicates the perspective of one side in a law-and-fact context that both sides have carefully constructed together. Listening to the other side argue and evaluating that argument is at least one half of the lawyer's role, while making one's own argument is the other and often lesser half.

So, no, lawyers have no problem hearing out the other side. Lawyers love it when you do the talking because while you talk, they get to listen and evaluate. Many lawyers feel that listening is a more-powerful skill than arguing. You can do far more than get a word in edgewise.

70

Eavesdroppers Beware

Question

I just found out that I can record telephone and in-person conversations using my smartphone. Boy, have I got some ideas to catch with their own words some of these rascals with whom I deal. Nothing wrong with that, is there?

Answer

Nothing other than potential federal and state crimes, and civil liability, depending on how you use the recording. Be very cautious in making secret recordings of others.

Your main concern should be federal and state wiretapping statutes. You probably think of wiretapping as placing an electronic recording device on someone else's phone line to listen in on a conversation to which you are not a known party. While courts may authorize law-enforcement officials to conduct investigations through wiretaps, when a private unauthorized person secretly records the calls of others, that person violates federal and state wiretap statutes. Violating the wiretap laws can result in criminal charge and conviction, incarceration, and fines, and also civil liability.

Yet wiretap laws have a greater reach than many realize. Federal law and state wiretap laws generally prohibit recording conversations to which the recorder or some other consenting person is a not a party, known as the one-party-consent rule. At least one person to the telephone conversation must know of and agree to the recording. That person could be you, the recorder, of course. Yet some states follow a stricter all-party-consent rule making it illegal to record a telephone conversation unless all parties know of and agree to the recording. Those laws are why you hear telephone service providers first caution that the company may monitor and record your call. They don't want to break these state laws. So you must know state law from state to state and be sure that you comply with the one- or all-party-consent rules, depending on the location (the state) of your callers.

Your other problem has to do with the privacy rights of the person whom you record. Many states recognize a right of individuals to prevent the public disclosure of private facts, when the disclosure would be highly offensive to the reasonable person. If, for instance, you uploaded to the internet a recording in which your caller made a private statement that, while appropriate to the subject of the private call, would nonetheless embarrass and highly offend the caller if the information became public, then you might have to pay that caller thousands of dollars in damages for the public disclosure. Individuals may regard as private any confidential information about their finances, relationships, sexual conduct, mental or physical health, criminal history, and many other areas.

If you have truly tired of not being able to trust the word of some who call you, and you have the need to rely on their communications, then consider informing them that you will be recording the conversation and that if they stay on the line, they are consenting to your using that recording to prove the communication's content. Think carefully about why you want to record something and how you would use the recording. Consult a lawyer if you feel that you really have the need to record secretly. Secret recordings, while potentially useful, can be hazardous.

And maybe another way to avoid the problem is not to deal with rascals.

69

Living Wills

Question

My adult daughter has been nagging me about being prepared for the worst. I don't know what her problem is. My diabetes, coronary artery disease, and emphysema aren't *that* bad. She says I need a living will. What's a living will?

Answer

You need someone close to you whom you have authorized and prepared to tell doctors what to do in case you cannot tell them.

You may be thinking that doctors don't need anyone telling them anything because they're the experts. They will do what they think best to do. Yet whether in ordinary care or medical crises, medicine often presents a range of options each of which carries certain benefits and risks. You have probably already been making important choices about your medical regimen for the three conditions you name. Doctors must inform you about those benefits and risks or may face malpractice liability for not getting your informed consent. In a medical crisis in which you were unable to tell doctors which option you prefer, the doctors would need to know your treatment preferences. Otherwise, the hospital might have to go to court to get an order regarding decisions over your treatment.

A living will is another name for an advance healthcare directive. An advance directive sets out your treatment preferences before you become mentally disabled by a medical crisis, when you still have the time and competent state of mind to think clearly about those preferences. Advance directives can be simple giving some general guides or elaborate going through specific scenarios. A well-designed advance directive and your adult daughter or another person close to you would help you think carefully about your commitments, preferences, and choices. Lawyers often help clients prepare and execute advance directives when executing estate-planning documents like trusts and wills. You would then keep your signed advance directive available to your medical care providers in your patient records.

Living wills are closely related to and sometimes identified as durable powers of attorney for healthcare, also known as patient designate for healthcare decisions. While a living will or advance directive expresses your treatment preferences, a healthcare power of attorney authorizes another trusted person such as your adult daughter to make treatment decisions for you according to your advance directive. Not only do doctors need to know your treatment preferences, they really need someone authorized by you with whom to discuss and weigh those options when you are no longer competent. You designate that person using the healthcare power of attorney. Some documents combine your treatment preferences (the advance directive) and the patient designate (the power of attorney) in a single document variously known by any of these names.

Hospitals will generally require a patient to execute a healthcare power of attorney if the patient has not already done so. They know how messy things can get without one. If you don't have a healthcare power of attorney when you reach the hospital in a medical crisis, the hospital may even ask you to complete one. States have varying requirements for a valid healthcare power of attorney. Some states require two witnesses to sign, while others may require witnessing and signature by a notary public and signed acceptance by your designate. Medical crises are not generally good times to be giving careful thought to executing helpful paperwork. Far better to complete an advance directive and healthcare power of attorney in advance.

So as confident as you are in your ability to manage your serious medical conditions, listen to your adult daughter. Be thoughtful not just to yourself but to her. Children and others who must make medical decisions for their parents or loved ones face daunting emotional and spiritual challenges. Give your daughter the help she needs, and you will be caring for her while you care for yourself.

68

Limited-Liability Heaven?

Question

Limited-liability-companies must be the best thing since sliced bread. When my company fails, I just start another one, and then another one, and another one, each one free of the prior one's debts. You lawyers are great! I'll never have to pay another business debt, right?

Answer

Sorry to disappoint you, but limited-liability companies are not your eternal ticket to debt-free heaven. The law is not nearly as foolish as that. While a limited-liability company can protect its owner-members from some liabilities, it is certainly no vehicle for turning successive business failures into personal success. You need a much better plan.

A limited-liability company is a newer corporate form that state legislatures across the country have authorized to supplement traditional business forms including the corporation and partnership. State legislatures approved limited-liability companies largely to achieve a tax advantage that business owners had long sought. In the simplest terms, corporations have the advantage of limiting the entity's liabilities to the corporation's assets. Yet without a special election, corporations must pay income tax at the corporate level. Shareholders pay income tax again on corporate dividends, meaning a double tax. Partnerships do not pay income tax (only the partners pay) but do not offer limited liability (all partners have liability). Limited-liability companies do not pay income tax but do provide limited liability, offering owner-members both advantages of fewer taxes and less liability. Consult your lawyer for the many subtleties and exceptions to this general description.

You ordinarily form a limited-liability company by filing articles of organization with the state and then adopting an operating agreement among the company's members. As members, you and the others who form the business with you decide your percentage membership interests in the business, simultaneously designating the company's manager. While you may wish to be the only member of your limited-liability company, federal and state tax authorities may treat a single-member limited-liability company differently from a multiple-member limited-liability company. You may find fewer advantages to a single-member limited-liability company than the usual multiple-member limited-liability company particularly when it comes to protecting the company from your individual creditors. Consult your lawyer for advice concerning forming and operating your limited-liability company.

The limited liability of a limited-liability company is not a perfect shield, nor should it be. State laws limit to the company liabilities that arise for company obligations. For example, if the company leases an office, vehicle, or piece of equipment but then defaults on the lease, the lessor may ordinarily sue only the company, not its owner-members. Yet lessors, banks or other lenders, suppliers, and others with whom your company does business may require your personal guarantee of company obligations. You may find it difficult or impossible to get credit, equipment, supplies, and other things necessary for your business without those personal guarantees or otherwise showing your company's financial responsibility. You would find it especially hard to get credit for your second company after your first company failed.

You may incur other personal liabilities in addition to guaranteed contract and credit obligations. Operating through a limited-liability company does not relieve you from your personal wrongs, even those wrongs that you commit in the course of the company's business. For instance, if you operated a company vehicle negligently causing another's injury, then you may well be liable to that individual, even as the company could also be liable for its owning and consenting to the use of its company vehicle. For another example, if you were to misrepresent the company's financial condition in order to attract credit, to sell the business, or for another purpose, and others suffered loss in reliance on your misrepresentation, then misrepresentation liability would extend to you (the perpetrator of the fraud) rather than be limited to the company. The shield of a limited-liability company protects members from company liabilities, not from liabilities that they personally create and incur through their own misconduct.

In sum, to start businesses successfully, you must have skill and plans. You just need a better plan for sustaining them. Consult a lawyer to help develop lawful options. And forget about your plan for serial failing limited-liability companies. Not only would you end up with no business and a very bad reputation, but you could also end up with some significant liabilities. Limited-liability companies are no limited-liability heaven.

67

Board to Death

Question

You lawyers must love serving on boards. Every board I've ever been on had a lawyer on it. Why do lawyers serve on so many school, nonprofit, corporate, and other committees and boards?

Answer

I bet you were glad that your boards had lawyers on them.

Boards govern organizations, not micro-managing but rather ensuring that the overall direction and integrity of the organization is sound. To govern an organization effectively, a board needs a range of views and skills. For example, a board often benefits by having industry insiders on it, those who know a lot about the field in which the organization operates. Boards also benefit by having financial expertise such as accountants and bankers can provide. Boards also benefit by having business, marketing, public-relations, and human-resources experts on them, and then perhaps experts in organizational development and strategy. The stronger the board, the stronger the organization. When an organization fails, you will sometimes see behind the failure an ineffective board.

Lawyers can have a little of each of the above skills. Lawyers can know at least a little of finance, business, marketing, public relations, human resources, strategy, and organizational development. Yet lawyers also know law, risk management, relationship management, and compliance. Board-member lawyers can alert organizations to legal, ethical, and other governance concerns that non-lawyers might miss, lacking a lawyer's legal training. Law school and law practice teach lawyers analytical skills that serve boards well. Lawyers know how to frame issues and opportunities for the organization, develop criteria, collect and evaluate evidence, and reach and justify sound conclusions. Lawyer skills closely match board responsibilities.

Lawyers are also good at board leadership. While not every lawyer on a board rises to the position of the board's chair, many do so. Trained in procedure, lawyers can be good at running board meetings openly and fairly. They know how to develop and carry out a meeting agenda. They know when to speak and when to listen. They know how to speak civilly while disagreeing and how to coax others to do so. They know how to foster helpful openness and dissent. Lawyers can set and maintain a necessary tone of rigorous discussion within a helpful tone of respect and civility. Lawyers can elevate the culture and performance of a board with their thoughtful insight, professional demeanor, stability in challenge, and general consistency.

While board service can be time-consuming, challenging, and even exhausting, lawyers do generally benefit through their board service. Many lawyers market their services solely or largely by word-of-mouth, through networks of current and former clients, and professional and social acquaintances. Board service brings lawyers into positive professional contact with professionals in other fields. Lawyers learn from and about those other professionals, while those other professionals get to know and trust the lawyer and the lawyer's knowledge and skill. Lawyers will seek out board and other community service both because it is the right thing to do and because it can expand their circle of professional acquaintances and influence. Lawyers are often better able to serve their own clients when they have the knowledge, perspective, reach, and influence that board service can bring.

Respect the lawyers who serve on your boards. And if you are ever on a board without a lawyer, then recruit one.

66

Freebies

Question

I've been asking you all these questions, one after another. You've answered every one of them without hesitation. Some of your answers are going to be very helpful to me. Do you ever tire of giving away free advice?

Answer

Free? You'll be getting my bill in the mail. Just kidding! Keep 'em coming, friend. Glad it's helpful to you.

You are right that counsel to clients is a lawyer's basic stock in trade. Lawyers do not make widgets, bake bread, set broken bones, or fix flat tires. They give counsel. Informed talk is largely their service, although they also draft documents, pleadings, and court papers, and advocate in court filings and at hearings, and then also negotiate, mediate, and do many other things promoting the interests of their clients. As you rightly suspect, many lawyers earn their keep by billing for the time that they spend giving counsel and performing other services. Yet lawyers certainly do not bill for every communication in which they are sharing their law knowledge and analysis. Lawyers often speak freely, sharing their evaluation and opinions with others whom they do not at that moment represent and will not be billing.

That said, when a lawyer is talking to you about your matter in an informal setting in which you have not actually paid or promised to pay the lawyer, the lawyer is still likely to owe you a duty of competence. In other words, the setting does not generally matter to the lawyer's duty to know and accurately apply the law to the matter about which the lawyer speaks. You may be at a party or on the golf course, but if the lawyer is opining on your matter, the lawyer likely needs to ensure that the advice is sound notwithstanding the informal setting. The duty rule has a few exceptions such as when the lawyer is representing your opponent. Don't rely on the advice of the other side's lawyer whose duties the lawyer owes to his or her own client, not you, the client's opponent. Yet in general, a lawyer's advice must be sound.

Even so, the kind of general answers that lawyers often give in informal out-of-office conversations, indeed of the kind that I have been sharing with you, are generally not sufficient to accomplish the things you might hope to achieve with a lawyer's advice. My general statements of law and its practice really only give you hints and guides as to what general direction your actions may best take. For any lawyer to give an informed opinion on your matter or any other matter would take you relating much more of your situation, goals, and interests, and then further take the lawyer's diligent investigation. Do not rely on websites, banter at social events, and other informal talk, even if the information that you glean comes from a highly skilled and knowledgeable lawyer. The lawyer may be doing his or her best to help but is likely not sufficiently informed to give you the counsel you need.

So, why do lawyers talk so freely? Part of their loquaciousness may simply be that lawyers are generally engaging talkers. Lawyers know a lot about a few things and a little about a lot of things, enough to be good company and a good source of general information. Another reason that lawyers will talk has to do with marketing or networking. Many lawyers do not advertise but instead find new clients by word of mouth, including their own word of mouth. If you meet a lawyer who seems naturally knowledgeable and willing to help, that lawyer may indeed be glad to have you retain him or her. Consider asking about engaging the lawyer's services. It never hurts to ask. The lawyer should give you a clearer idea of the lawyer's practice, fees, and interest or willingness. You need not accept the lawyer's offer to help. Take the lawyer's card, ask the lawyer for a reference or two among current or former clients, and go check the lawyer out.

Oh, and by the way, lawyers also do substantial pro bono service for clients who cannot afford a lawyer. Once again, it never hurts to ask.

65

Overbilling

Question

I just got a bill from my lawyer that was more than twice what I expected and probably triple what it should have been. I am so angry at this connivance that I can hardly see straight. Do all lawyers overbill?

Answer

No, overbilling is rare. Lawyers who do so lose clients.

First, appreciate that a larger-than-expected bill does not necessarily mean that the lawyer was greedy or dishonest. Instead, a client receiving a larger-than-expected bill often has to do with a failure to communicate adequately about the project's scope. In other words, the lawyer may have done more for you than you wished or expected. If the two of you had communicated better, then you might have received the work and bill you expected. Lawyers will often confirm for you the scope of the work not just orally when meeting with you about your matter but in a written fee agreement.

114

Writing down what work you have authorized helps your lawyer clarify and confirm for you what to expect in billing. In certain cases, conduct rules require lawyers to provide clients with written fee agreements. Even when not technically required, written fee agreements are generally very good ideas for both client and lawyer. Fee issues can be complex, making a writing helpful to confirm and record agreement. If you had a written fee agreement with your lawyer, then go back and read it again. If you do not understand it or if you think that your lawyer did not comply with it, then respectfully call those issues to your lawyer's attention. The writing may matter more than your expectation.

A larger-than-expected bill can also have to do with the risk of your matter. Lawyers often cannot always predict with certainty and control the amount of time that they will have to devote to your matter. Unpredictability is a particular problem with litigation when the opposing side has a lot to say about the matter's scope and thus its cost. Your problem may have been more unpredictable and less within your lawyer's control than you expected. You and your lawyer could likely have discussed those risks before you authorized the work. Even in risky matters, though, lawyers will sometimes offer a client a fixed fee, in effect accepting the risk so that the client can rely on a known and affordable cost. Unlike clients, lawyers can often spread the risk of individual matters across many of those matters, so that one matter that takes less work helps pay for another matter that takes more work. Next time, ask your lawyer about a fixed fee.

A larger-than-expected bill can also mean that you received a more valuable service and result than you expected. Lawyers must only charge authorized and reasonable fees. Just because a lawyer can provide more valuable service for you than you expected does not mean that a lawyer may do so and expect you to pay for it. Yet if you authorized the work, the fee was reasonable, and you got more than you bargained to receive, then you may not have much about which to complain. Ask your lawyer to explain the value of the service that the lawyer

115

provided. If the bill was twice what you expected but the service three times more valuable to you, then you might want to reconsider your anger over it.

In the end, though, lawyers rely on their reputation. Most lawyers care about how a client feels about a bill. Happy clients make for more clients. Just because you got an unexpectedly large bill does not mean that you must pay for it. Talk to your lawyer, not in anger but reasonably. Ask whether your lawyer exceeded the project's authorized scope or encountered an undisclosed but predictable risk. If so, then your lawyer should probably be thinking about reducing your bill. Conduct rules prohibit lawyers from charging excessive fees. Yet even if you received in scope and value exactly what you authorized, and received a fair and authorized billing, your lawyer may recognize that better communication could have avoided the issue. Lawyers do adjust billings.

Listen carefully to your lawyer, though, because chances are pretty good that you received the service and bill you authorized. After all, lawyers usually know contracts better than clients. Do yourself a favor: don't start the conversation with anger.

64

Good and Bad Lawyers

Question

Twice I've had the help of lawyers with important matters. The first time, the lawyer was fantastic—smart, encouraging, supportive, prompt, fair, and effective. The second time, the lawyer was a wreck—discouraging, late, and ineffective. Next time I need a lawyer, how do I get the former rather than the latter?

Answer

The three professionals you always want to be good and never bad are your doctor, dentist, and lawyer.

You have several ways to ensure that you retain only consistently good lawyers. First, make your own judgment. Look closely at everything you can see about the lawyer including the lawyer's advertising, brochures, letterhead, and business card. Does the lawyer present a clear, consistent, and positive professional identity? The lawyer who cannot get his or her proverbial act together on these lawyer basics may not be able to help you with yours. Do the same with your initial consultation

117

with the lawyer. Many lawyers offer free first meetings, especially if you indicate that you want to meet to decide whether to retain the lawyer. How does the lawyer handle the meeting? Did the lawyer seem attentive, caring, and knowledgeable? A lawyer should be able to convey to you, both orally and in writing, a strong sense of confidence in the lawyer's skill.

While making your own assessment of your lawyer's competence, look for the assessments of others. One way to find a good lawyer is to ask family members and trusted friends. Another way is to ask other lawyers. Lawyers hesitate to recommend anyone other than a clearly competent lawyer because if the lawyer whom they recommend commits malpractice, then the recommender may also be liable. Moreover, many lawyers depend on their referral networks. If one lawyer refers you to another lawyer, the second lawyer may make sure to treat you well in order to keep the referrals coming. Professionals are accountable to one another, just as they are accountable to you. Current and former clients can also be good evaluators of their lawyers. Ask the lawyer whom you are thinking of retaining if the lawyer has a client or former client whom you can contact for a reference.

You can also check your state's bar association online to see if the lawyer's license is current and if the licensing authority has ever disciplined the lawyer. Be sure that those public records indicate that your lawyer is in good standing. Most lawyers never suffer any license-related discipline. If the records indicate one or more disciplines of your lawyer, then read those accounts carefully before deciding whether to retain the lawyer. Discipline officials would not have reinstated the lawyer after discipline unless those officials believed the lawyer was competent to practice law, but again, you should if you wish be able to find another lawyer who has no record of discipline. Local bar associations can be another good source for referrals and referral information. Call your local bar association to ask.

118

You can also find lawyer-rating services online. Some are longstanding, well-researched, and generally reliable, while others are less reliable or even unreliable. Rating services can exaggerate the qualifications of some lawyers, particularly those lawyers who devote significant resources to building ratings, while under-representing or even misrepresenting the qualifications of other lawyers. Newer lawyers who may be highly competent and eager to serve you may lack the ratings that senior lawyers built up over time, while some of those senior lawyers may no longer have the knowledge or skill to be as effective as they once were. Be cautious in relying on ratings. Be sure the information on which you rely is current and sound.

Finally, ask your lawyer if the lawyer has malpractice insurance. Your lawyer should have that insurance, which protects both the lawyer *and you* against the lawyer's malpractice. Some states require lawyers to disclose their malpractice insurance, while other states do not require disclosure, but any lawyer should be willing to tell you. Some lawyers will even require other lawyers to provide them with a current copy of their malpractice insurance before referring any clients to them or co-counseling any matter with them. Any lawyer can make a mistake, although good ones make fewer of them. In the rare event of malpractice, you want insurance to make you whole.

So, in with the good, out with the bad. As obvious and sound as these steps are, few clients take them. More clients should. Don't let your lawyer choose you. You choose your lawyer. You wouldn't choose an incompetent plumber. Be sure you choose just as wisely or more so when choosing your lawyer.

63

Is Law School *that* Hard?

Question

I always hear the same thing that law school is the hardest thing you lawyers have ever done. Law school cannot really be *that* hard, can it?

Answer

Well, yes, it *can* be *that* hard. The difficulty may not be quite the same as, say, childbirth, but then again, law school lasts a lot longer and has some similarly, shall we say, *intense* moments.

Oddly enough, law school is hard physically, certainly not like military training or even being a day laborer, but hard physically nonetheless. The physical part of law school has to do with the sheer quantity of reading, listening, concentrating, recalling, analyzing, speaking, writing, and associated mental effort. To many people, mental effort has no physical aspect to it—probably because they have never thought as hard and as long as law students routinely think. At some point though, usually after a few hours, concentrating becomes physical. Study wearies the body, not just the mind. Sitting down to read is generally pleasurable. Yet try sitting down to read not just for an hour, nor two or four hours, but eight or ten hours. And not just to read but to read *and remember*. Now you get an idea of the physical challenge.

The mental challenge of law school has to do with more than just memory. Law school involves some rote memory. At some level, you just have to know the three elements of battery, four elements of negligence, five conditions for adverse possession, and a myriad of other detail. Yet other than for law school exams and bar exams, lawyers do not necessarily walk around with a lot of law crammed into their heads. A lawyer's knowledge is functional knowledge, not rote knowledge. Law school is hard mentally because law students are learning to *think*, not just to memorize. Learning to use your brain requires more than just firing up a few more neurons. The kind of deep and structured thought that law school teaches law students actually forms new mental structures. The webs of dendrites that connect brain cells actually grow through the constant use and effort of law school.

To grow in mental power requires that law students spend a lot of time in what educators call the *zone of proximal development.* You know that burning pain in the muscles that tells you that you are getting physically stronger from intense exercise but at the same time makes you sick to your stomach? Well, law school pushes students into a similar but *mental* zone that, while necessary for mental growth, can seem instead like the mental pain of bewilderment and confusion. Law students are generally quite bright and confident, but push them in class and other studies well beyond their mental comfort zone, and they can experience speechlessness, embarrassment, and even some humiliation. After all, public speaking is among the worst of people's fears. Yet law students speak frequently, often without choice and when they would far rather not speak, in front of larger numbers of very smart and critical fellow students.

Again, law school is not like military training. No one holds you underwater longer than you can hold your breath, makes you huddle outside for days in a cold rain, or deprives you of food, sleep, and other physical comfort. Yet the mental difficulty of law school, constantly subjecting the student to successively more difficult mental challenges, can still have adverse effects. Law students report higher levels of depression and substance abuse, for instance, especially when without family and social support.

The biggest challenge of law school though can be its spiritual challenge, the challenge that it presents to making purpose and meaning of the things and relationships around you. No other education is quite like it. A law degree is in many respects the pinnacle degree, proof that one has made comprehensive sense of how people ought to relate best to one another in every good and bad thing that they do under the sun. Conscious and responsible life is simply that profound that one must dig deeply to discover its stronger meanings. It would be a shame if law school was not hard because it would then have left something undiscovered. Law school should be hard. You wouldn't want a half-made lawyer representing you in your most-important legal matters, would you?

So next time you see a law student, give him or her a word of encouragement. Law school *is that* hard.

62

The Bar Exam

Question

I hear law students groan about the upcoming bar exam. I am not sure what a bar exam is, but hey, for as good as you lawyers have it, and for as much as we pay you, I figure that you deserve the bar exam, right!?

Answer

No one deserves a bar exam. You wouldn't wish it on your worst enemy.

Actually, the bar exam can be a refreshing challenge, if only we had the right attitude about it. When else in life do you get to put everything else aside for about eight weeks of intense planning and total devotion to one very difficult object? No, I do not mean preparing for your wedding. The bar exam takes that kind of total devotion. Nearly every examinee who fails the bar exam will say the same thing, that they did not take it seriously enough. Some very smart, well-known, and powerful people have failed bar exams. They did so not because they were not smart enough but because they did not or could not devote sufficient time to preparing for it.

Passing the bar takes setting everything aside to study for it intensely for a period at least a little longer than seems human. While the prominent special bar-preparation courses tend to last six to eight weeks leading up to the exam, wiser examinees will spend hundreds of hours preparing for the bar over a longer period, say, six months or so. The point is that no one wants to fail the bar—and have to do it all over again. Failing the bar can be embarrassing, although it need not be. Failing actually puts an examinee in some pretty good company. Worse than any embarrassment, failing can delay employment as a lawyer for another six months. The bar exam happens only twice a year. Examinees who do not pass the first time must wait for the next exam, which is probably a good thing given the planning and effort that successful examination takes. No one should have to suffer it twice within six months.

The bar exam, a little different from state to state, is typically a two-day test of a lawyer's law knowledge and skill. Nearly all bar exams administer the same national battery of multiple-choice questions. Most bar exams then have written essay questions on a range of subjects, many of them fitted to the particular state's law. Many bar exams include a skills portion involving reviewing file materials and drafting documents. With rare exceptions, lawyers must pass a bar exam to gain their first law license. Officials license lawyers from state to state. After gaining a license by examination in one state, a lawyer may be able to gain a license in another state by experience rather than re-examination, or by a shorter examination, depending on the involved states. A good number of lawyers though must take the bar exam again later in a career when practicing within a new state.

Pass rates vary from state to state. On the nation's harder exams, only a little more than half of examinees pass. On less-hard exams (to avoid calling any exam *easier*), better than 80% of examinees will pass. No matter the rate, a good number of examinees still fail. Many will persist and pass later, while a few others try the bar exam only once. They may already have a different career in which the law degree, knowledge, and skills are helpful but in which they do not practice law. Having taken their medicine, they decide not to pursue the license after all. The saddest situations are those in which a skilled and knowledgeable law graduate keeps trying and trying but just cannot muster the unusual testing-taking skills that the bar exam requires. Unlicensed lawyers must not practice law but may find much meaningful work as law clerks and legal assistants or pursuing the many law-related fields.

While every licensed lawyer must at one time or another have thought that there must be a better way to licensure, the bar exam is nonetheless a useful rite of passage. The law profession, after all, takes the character of a fellowship, almost of a secret society, entry to which the bar exam makes the perfect sentinel.

61

Indigent Defense

Question

I hear all the time about people getting a free lawyer when charged with a crime. What gives with *that*? I thought criminals were supposed to have a hard time of it, not an easy time. Do they get free parking, too?

Answer

Well, no free parking, and not always a free lawyer, but sometimes an appointed and paid-for lawyer.

The Supreme Court held decades ago that constitutional due process requires that the criminally charged who face the prospect of incarceration but cannot afford a lawyer get an appointed lawyer. Criminal charges are serious and complex business. Even relatively sophisticated, highly educated defendants can find themselves overwhelmed when facing criminal charges. Even if they had the peace and clarity of mind to address their own defense, their lack of legal training in criminal procedure would generally make them utterly incapable of mounting a defense against the prosecution's sophistication and government

126

resources. Remember, not everyone charged with crime is guilty. Fundamental fairness requires that you have a lawyer's help when you face jail or prison. Without counsel, many more innocent persons would spend time in jail or prison for crimes that they did not commit.

If you cannot afford a lawyer to contest criminal charges that may result in your incarceration, then taxpayers pay for the lawyer to represent you. The right to counsel does not simply mean that if you can afford a lawyer, you get a lawyer. The Supreme Court has held that the right to counsel means you get a lawyer under some circumstances whether you can afford a lawyer or not. Oh, someone pays the lawyer. In that sense, the lawyer is not free. Depending on the court and location, either federal, state, or local indigent-defense programs pay the lawyer. Those programs of course require public funding, which ultimately means for the most part taxpayer funding. Taxpayers generally foot the bill, just like they foot the bill for most other government programs and services.

Lawyers who represent the indigent may work on salary for a public-defender organization or may instead be in private practice in their own firm. Private-practice lawyers who accept assignments may have signed up on a list of random draws for those assignments, qualified for assignments through a special program, or contracted with the funding agency for assignments. In any such case, lawyers who accept indigent-defense assignments are generally not making substantial fees on that work. Public coffers are not so rich as even to pay lawyers their going rates for private defense work with paying clients. Rather, lawyers taking assignments often work for significantly reduced hourly rates or relatively small fixed fees. The lower rates can affect the time that a lawyer is able to devote to an indigent client's matter and thus the quality of the representation.

More than just the criminally charged get the advantage of assigned defense counsel. Other indigent litigants get a paid-for lawyer, too. Think of those matters most important to a litigant beyond the litigant's freedom, and you may find authority for assigned counsel. Termination of parental rights is one such example. The state or local agency will generally assign a lawyer to represent the indigent parent who is about to lose parental rights to a child in an abuse or neglect proceeding. Notice, though, that only the most-serious matters warrant assigned counsel. Assigned counsel is generally not available for civil matters involving only money, even large sums of money.

The assigned-counsel system may at first blush seem a little coddling, but it definitely is not. Government is fallible. Simply because one is poor does not mean that one should suffer for the government's overreach or mistakes. As strange as it may seem to some, we should be glad for this fundamental of due process.

60

Despising the Client or Cause

Question

Hey, I saw that you represented that monster who escaped from jail and killed a police officer before getting caught. I know that the court appointed you, but couldn't you have refused? At least he got the life in prison that he deserved.

Answer

No, a lawyer generally cannot refuse an appointment when qualified and available to represent an indigent defendant. Lawyers do accept court appointment to represent defendants whose actions and character they despise, sometimes at significant personal and professional cost.

Lawyers take a public oath in court when they receive their license. While the oaths vary some from state to state, they routinely include the commitment not to turn away clients, whether or not indigent, who cannot find a lawyer to represent them. Lawyers hold a special privilege in the nature of keys to the courtroom. For all to receive justice, lawyers must not deny those keys to some while offering them to others. The courtroom is a forbidding place where one needs the help of a lawyer. Simply because the matter involves something repugnant does not necessarily mean that the lawyer may deny the client competent representation. The monsters need representation as much, indeed often more so, than the saints. We judge ourselves as much by the justice that we offer to the criminal as by the justice we offer to the saint.

Lawyers generally get to pick their clients. Lawyers do not have to take every client and matter that comes their way. If a lawyer has too many matters, or is cutting back toward retirement, or has decided not to handle certain cases, then the lawyer may decline a representation. Lawyers choose clients as much as clients choose lawyers. Many lawyers do no criminal-defense work at all. Many other lawyers handle criminal-defense matters only of a certain type, or in a certain court, or for certain clients. Lawyers generally get to shape their law practices, as long as they can find sufficient clients willing to pay them for their services.

Yet some clients, lawyers must consider representing, when no other lawyer would. With the privilege of holding the keys to justice comes responsibility for ensuring that all have access to justice. In any one community, only a few lawyers may have the skill, standing, character, and resources to represent a particularly difficult or repugnant client in a particularly egregious matter. Killing a police officer, committing sexual assaults on minors, and similarly hideous acts repel lawyers just as they do others. Lawyers feel real emotions of the kind that others would feel, when confronting the reality of those terrible crimes. Still, some lawyers have the skill and character to set emotions aside enough to concentrate on the legal tasks at hand that will ensure a fair trial. Judges know who those lawyers are and will call on those lawyers to handle these cases.

Like most any rule, a lawyer's duty to represent the undesirable client who has no other representation does have its exceptions. One exception is for undue hardship. If the client's case is so overwhelming in scope that it would put the lawyer out of practice, then the lawyer may decline. Only larger firms with teams of lawyers can handle some particularly burdensome matters. Another exception is when the client or cause is so repugnant that the lawyer will be unable to perform competently. We all have our limits. The profession would not expect a lawyer who was sexually abused as a child to represent an alleged child abuser or a Jewish lawyer to represent a Nazi defendant— although as extraordinary as it seems, some lawyers have been able to do so.

The negative effect on a lawyer's reputation is not an exception to the duty rule though. Representing a client does not mean that a lawyer agrees with the client's conduct or even the client's cause. Yet the public may misconstrue the representation that way, hurting the lawyer's reputation with the public. Lawyers know better. Within the bar, the reputation of a lawyer who takes on a difficult client and cause increases rather than suffering. Lawyer chatter in the courthouse hallways will fall silent in respect as the burdened lawyer passes. Take enough of these difficult matters, and respectful silence can turn to something like reverence. Lawyers have few better ways to make a professional reputation than to offer the courthouse keys to the lease among us. Ask Atticus Finch.

59

Whoa, Nelly

Question

I had a little project for my lawyer to do, one that should have taken no more than an hour and cost a couple hundred bucks. A week later, I got a 20-page legal-research memorandum and $2,500 bill. Whoa, Nelly. How do I keep my lawyer from doing more than the lawyer should?

Answer

Make a clear agreement in advance on the project's scope and cost. Then get your lawyer's commitment to hold to the project budget or notify you in advance for your approval to go outside the initial project scope or estimated cost.

Predicting just what a legal matter may entail can be difficult. A surgeon does not always know what's inside until the surgery commences. A mechanic does not always know all the repairs that a vehicle requires until after fixing the most obvious problems and finding that the vehicle still does not run. Similarly, lawyers cannot always foresee the scope of a legal project at its outset when they have little more than the client's limited information.

If the matter involves commencing civil litigation for the client, then the client may not have foreseen the defenses or counterclaims that the opposing party may raise. If the matter involves documenting a transaction, then the client may not have foreseen all of the issues that due diligence raises. Legal matters have their uncertainties, each of which can affect the project costs.

Yet a good discussion of project parameters and an agreement to communicate before exceeding estimated project costs can reduce the risk of unexpected matters and, worse, unexpectedly high legal bills. While legal matters inevitably involve uncertainties, lawyers can be pretty good at foreseeing typical project courses and predicting average project costs. Any one matter may take a completely unexpected and unforeseeable turn, busting the project budget, but most matters will fall within a reasonable and foreseeable range of expected courses and outcomes. Discuss that range with your lawyer. Get the lawyer to commit to a project budget that you can understand and with which you can live. Moreover, get the lawyer to commit in writing not to exceed the budget without notifying you first and getting your approval. The bill may not ultimately be what you like, but at least you will not be surprised.

You may even have a better course than being at the mercy of your own project's uncertainties. Lawyers in some fields are increasingly able and willing to work from fixed fees. With a fixed fee, you pay one price for your project, while the lawyer bears the risk of the project turning out to be more complex or difficult than expected. Lawyers can spread those risks across multiple matters. You might pay a little more for a fixed fee than if you had offered to pay an hourly fee and your matter had turned out to be especially simple. But then you never quite know for certain. If you cannot or do not wish to take the risk of your matter turning out to be more difficult and expensive, then talk to your lawyer about a fixed fee. Some lawyers and law firms are even handling complex civil litigation (an inherently uncertain area) for fixed fees.

The lack of transparency in pricing creates problems for consumers purchasing legal services. When you choose a cable service, you can compare options and costs, and get just what you are willing to purchase. The same is true with your cell phone contract, motor-vehicle insurance, and rent or mortgage. Lawyers on the other hand tend not to be so clear in the options you may have and the costs associated with those options. In the end, though, you the consumer have the power. Find a lawyer who is willing to discuss project options, scope, and costs with you and then to commit in writing to your parameters. Know what you are getting, and know what you will pay for it. Help your lawyer understand and appreciate that when it comes to billing, you don't want any surprises.

58

It's Not Easy Being Crazy

Question

I just saw on the news another criminal pleading insanity to one of those horrible crimes. I mean, when you pull out the gun, point it at someone, and pull the trigger, isn't that enough proof of the crime? What's with this insanity defense?

Answer

First, convicting the certifiably crazy should make anyone more than a little uncomfortable. A deranged mind is different from a guilty mind and a deranged act different from a guilty act. And second, just because a defendant pleads insanity doesn't mean the court will find the defendant insane. While horribly insane acts should make us feel very uncomfortable, the insanity defense actually makes much legal sense.

Serious crimes have a mental component. Shooting someone deliberately is a much more serious crime than shooting someone accidentally. The distinction between deliberate crimes and unintentional conduct requires that the law consider the quality of the defendant's state of mind. Given the nature and prevalence of mental illness, and the distorted nature of crime itself, sometimes the defendant's state of mind is so deranged as not to fit neatly into categories of deliberate intent or unintended accident, guilt or innocence. Schizophrenia, which mental-health professionals define as a person's inability to distinguish the imagined from the real, is an example. How could we convict a schizophrenic of murder for shooting the mailman when the schizophrenic genuinely thought that he was petting the cat?

The law defines insanity different from mental-health professionals define any particular mental disorder. Just because someone has schizophrenia or depression or bipolar disorder does not mean that they have a license to kill. The law looks to the quality of the defendant's state of mind approaching and at the moment of the crime, not to the peculiar medical diagnosis. The law will convict a schizophrenic of murder if the schizophrenic actually perceived the real nature of the horrible act. To put the point another way, mental-health professionals do not diagnose patients as *insane*. They have their own diagnostic lexicon and quite-different therapeutic purposes for giving labels to their patients' conditions. *Insanity* is a legal term, not a medical term.

The public is generally aware of some of the more-infamous instances of insanity ameliorating the crime. John Hinckley shot and almost killed President Reagan reportedly to impress actress Jodie Foster whom he had pursued and stalked without success. That's insanity. He has remained institutionalized since but with progressively longer supervised releases. Outcry over the not-guilty-by-reason-of-insanity verdict led to new federal laws making the defense more difficult to establish. Mark David Chapman's lawyers asserted an insanity defense after he shot and killed John Lennon and then remained peacefully at the dead man's side reading *Catcher in the Rye*, but Chapman withdrew the defense and pled guilty, reportedly when God told him to do so. He remains in prison despite having served the minimum life-sentence time.

State laws actually vary considerably on the nature and effects of an insanity defense. Defending successfully on an insanity defense does not mean that the defendant goes free. Rather, the court may commit the insane defendant to a secure mental-health facility that to the normal mind would look and feel a lot like jail. And depending on the defendant's condition and recovery, the defendant may remain institutionalized for just as long as or longer than the defendant would have remained in prison if convicted of the crime. Some states reject the insanity-defense label, calling the condition *guilty but mentally ill.* The effect in each case may generally be the same that the law will then institutionalize and treat the defendant more so than punish the defendant in prison or jail. Punishment makes little sense to the mentally ill person who does not understand the crime.

Oh, and one last note. It can be easy to confuse an insanity defense with the defendant not being competent to stand trial. In some instances, the defendant may have been plenty sane at the time of the incident to commit the crime with the required state of mind, but the incident itself or something that happened to the defendant later so deranged the defendant's mind that the defendant cannot participate meaningfully at trial. How, for instance, does one mount a defense to a charge while in a coma, or while catatonic, or while so hallucinatory as not to be able to trust or understand one's own lawyer? In those cases, the court may simply have mental-health providers hold the defendant in a secure facility as long as it takes for the defendant to regain enough sense to face the criminal trial.

The mind is a mysterious and delicate thing. The criminal-justice system must deal with it on compromise terms. Insanity and incompetence may seem like lame excuses when placed up against a horrible crime, but they make their own sense of profoundly difficult, sad, and even tragic situations.

57

Intoxication Defense

Question

My buddy got stone drunk, walked into a stranger's house, turned on the stereo, and fell asleep on the couch. Next thing he knew, he was in jail for criminal trespassing. They can't convict a man for trespassing when he's out-of-his-mind drunk, can they?

Answer

So, let's see. Everything's legal as long as you're drunk enough not to appreciate the wrong you're committing?

You can see the problem that the law would have with excusing crimes based on intoxication. Trespass of the type that you described is clearly a crime. The incident you described, while funny-sounding in one sense, may have deeply alarmed residents of the home including women and children. Home invasions, even when relatively innocent, can cause longer-lasting mental fright and shock particularly when the residents are already susceptible for other reasons. Worse harm could have resulted if the residents had mistaken your friend for a threat to

138

their physical safety. And defendants have raised intoxication defenses to much more serious crimes right up to murder.

The intoxication defense is indeed a problematic one for the law. The problem is that intoxication is generally voluntary. If one gets drunk on purpose, then it seems unfair to excuse the less-purposeful ribaldry that follows. The law certainly does not want to encourage public drunkenness. It is not prudery to say that drunkenness is a scourge for law and society. Thousands die in drunk-driving accidents. Drunken rages cause thousands more domestic-violence injuries. Alcohol and substance abuse contributes to job loss, divorce, physical ailments, and any number of other societal ills having profoundly negative impacts on individuals, families, and children.

The law's challenge with the intoxication defense is to set the bar high enough to recognize these deleterious effects of drunkenness and to discourage it, while still respecting that some crimes require a certain guilty state of mind. The law divides specific-intent crimes from general-intent crimes. To commit the former, one must know and intend the wrong or harm. To commit the latter, one need only intend the conduct without necessarily knowing and intending the harm. While laws vary from state to state, extreme intoxication is more commonly a defense to specific-intent crimes than general-intent crimes. In other words, you might get away with some things but not other things. For example, extreme intoxication might reduce a first-degree-murder charge to a second-degree-murder conviction. The extreme intoxicant would not have premeditated and deliberated over the crime.

The policy behind the law is important. Courts can be quicker to recognize defenses based on involuntary intoxication than based on self-intoxication. When someone purposefully imbibes hoping to get so drunk as unwittingly to commit a crime (yes, people do such incredibly stupid things), then the courts are likely to convict despite the intoxication. Yet when someone falls under the influence without intending to do so, for example by

139

consuming a spiked drink at a party, state laws may treat the resulting state of mind more like insanity than culpable voluntary intoxication. Involuntary intoxication may more likely be a defense not only to specific-intent crimes but also to general-intent crimes. In the event of a conviction, intoxication may also mitigate the punishment, particularly when the intoxication was involuntary or otherwise less culpable.

Moral of the story? Don't drink and commit crimes. Your friend is in trouble.

56

Copping a Plea

Question

My son-in-law got arrested and charged for something he didn't do, although he was probably doing some other things for which they could have arrested and charged him. Now his public defender wants him to plead guilty to a lesser charge. Why are defense lawyers always trying to get their clients to cop a plea?

Answer

Control. Trials are inherently uncertain. A plea on favorable terms is often better than an unpredictable trial result.

Evidence often supports multiple charges, some more serious than others. A single criminal charge may have several required elements. If the evidence for one of those elements is missing or uncertain, then the remaining elements for which the evidence is strong or even uncontested may still make a lesser-included charge. First-degree murder may become second-degree murder or just manslaughter if evidence of deliberation is uncertain or absent. Attempted murder may become assault and battery if evidence of the probable harm is weak or uncertain. Crimes of

141

intent may become crimes of recklessness or negligence if evidence of intent is weak or absent.

Given the complexity and layered nature of criminal charges, guilty pleas to lesser offenses are nothing unusual. Most criminal charges result in plea agreements. Prosecutors and courts have nowhere near the time, staffing, and resources to try every charge. They expect most cases to resolve in plea deals, and most cases routinely do so resolve. Defendants charged with crimes accept plea offers for several reasons. Substantial evidence of guilt is one of those reasons. When evidence supports a higher charge, pleading to a lesser charge that carries a lesser penalty can make quite a bit of sense. The system of plea bargaining can be quite humane in that respect that it gives criminal defendants a degree of mercy that would not be available if the defendant stood on every procedural right.

Plea bargaining can be especially attractive when considering the possible penalties following conviction. Defendants can have enormous reasons to avoid incarceration, for instance, such as to save a job, child custody, or marriage. Pleading to a lesser offense that would result in a sentence without incarceration may be distasteful and embarrassing, but the alternative of facing jail or prison time while losing one's job, spouse, and kids could make the lesser plea quite a bit more attractive. Defendants plead guilty not only to preserve their employment, family relationships, and freedom but to save a professional license, save trial time and expense, and in some cases to avoid state prison in favor of local jail. A guilty plea is not a guarantee of a lenient sentence but can certainly go a long way toward gaining the sentencing judge's confidence that the defendant accepts appropriate responsibility for the crime.

You are right though to be concerned about an unjustified charge. Prosecutors have duties not to over-charge beyond what the evidence would support simply to leverage a plea to a lesser offense. Your son-in-law should have some procedural protections against unjustified charges. Defense lawyers can test the evidence for a charge at the preliminary examination and by motions to dismiss. Courts should dismiss charges for which the prosecution has no admissible evidence. Your son-in-law should not have to plead to any charge simply to avoid a charge for which the prosecution has no evidence.

So on the whole, your son-in-law's experience could be typical. Lawyers can get a bad reputation for urging clients to accept pleas. We like to think that our lawyers will go to battle for us, and indeed they should. Yet be careful interfering with the lawyer's advice to your son-in-law. You might not know everything that your son-in-law's lawyer knows. Control over the outcome may be your son-in-law's best strategy, particularly when a plea includes a diversion program, expungement, or other special relief from the sentence or conviction. Plea bargaining can be a wise approach.

55

In for Life, or Not

Question

I keep hearing about criminals sentenced to life in prison getting out long before the end of their life. I thought life in prison meant life in prison. How does the law get around that?

Answer

A life sentence should (and generally does) mean a sentence for as long as the convicted person lives. Yet a sentence for life does not necessarily mean spending life *in prison*. It may mean spending most of one's life in prison and then living the remainder of one's life under parole terms that could readily result in a permanent return to prison.

Judges sentence convicted criminals according to the applicable federal or state laws. Depending on the applicable law, some crimes like first-degree murder may require life sentences, while other crimes like armed robbery, rape, or child abuse may make life sentences discretionary with the judge. Where discretion exists, judges often look at the crime's reprehensibility, meaning just how bad it was. While the laws vary considerably, a life sentence generally does mean a sentence that lasts for the convicted person's natural life. It could also mean spending the rest of one's life in prison. Yet those laws routinely require that the judge set a minimum term along with the life sentence. The convicted person must generally serve that minimum term, such as 21 years or 25 years, before being eligible for parole.

Parole eligibility does not guarantee release. Far from it. Parole boards routinely deny release to criminals whom the board determines continue to represent a threat to society. Parole boards are not often known for their compassion. They have been known at parole hearings to take small prison tickets and offenses over many years of incarceration, or misplaced words suggesting poor attitude from the inmate, as indications that the inmate is not yet sufficiently rehabilitated. Victims and families of victims may also effectively oppose parole. Some victims and family members have long and painful memories. Judges, too, may have the authority under applicable law to prevent release on parole, by entering a whole-life order along with the life sentence. A whole-life order would prevent the convicted person's release by parole.

Reports suggest that about 1 in 10 prison inmates is serving a life sentence, while about 1 in 4 is serving life without parole. If rehabilitation is the goal, then life sentences may work. Among those life-sentence inmates who gain release on parole, only about 1 in 5 suffers re-arrest for crime within the first three years after release, while about 2 of 3 suffer re-arrest within the first three years for all released inmates. The cost is not cheap, though. Reports suggest a public price tag of about $1 million per life sentence. The length of life sentences has also increased from around 21 years to 29 years with the stiffening of sentencing laws. About seven states have over 1,000 lifers each, while six states prohibit parole for any convicted persons sentenced to life in prison. Data also suggests that even where available to lifers under state law, parole is less frequent than it once was.

Interestingly, judges can sentence criminals whom the court convicts of multiple crimes to separate periods of incarceration for each crime. Usually, judges allow the periods of incarceration to run all at one time so that the convicted person effectively serves only as much time as the longest sentence. Yet sometimes, often in the most egregious of cases, judges will order the sentences to run consecutively (one after another) rather than concurrently (overlapping). In those instances, the sentences can accumulate to more than one-hundred years. Sentences of that extraordinary proportion should satisfy anyone's thirst for retribution.

54

Death as a One-Way Street

Question

The news just showed another triple axe murderer getting a life sentence — three hots and a cot for this menace who should have gotten the electric chair for committing multiple grisly killings. Whatever happened to an eye for an eye, and a tooth for a tooth?

Answer

Whether the death penalty applies depends on the murders' circumstance and place. You might have had your way in another case or place.

The criminal law of murder is generally state rather than federal law, although some federal laws can apply in special situations. Some states recognize the death penalty, while others do not. Federal law provides for the death penalty in certain cases, but officials prosecute most murder cases under state rather than federal law. So depending on the state, the death penalty might have been available in the case about which you heard. The law calls the death penalty *capital punishment* and a crime

147

warranting the death penalty a *capital offense*. *Capital* refers to one's head, making the death penalty the equivalent of losing one's head.

The most-common ground for the death penalty is first-degree murder, but federal and state crimes in which the death penalty is available go well beyond murder. Federal capital offenses include treason, espionage (spying), mailing injurious articles intending to cause death, bank robbery causing death, and dozens of other offenses such as drug trafficking, child abuse, and carjacking when they also include murder. While the number of states recognizing the death penalty changes frequently, 32 states currently do so, all of them for first-degree murder, and 11 for crimes other than murder including treason, espionage, drug trafficking, and aircraft hijacking. Notice the seriousness of these crimes. The Supreme Court has ruled that the death penalty may only apply to crimes to which it is proportional punishment.

In states where the death penalty is available for certain crimes, whether the convicted person will actually get the death penalty may depend on several factors typically relating to the heinousness of the particular crime. Committing the crime is alone not necessarily sufficient to warrant the death penalty. The death penalty may require the kind of horrific conduct and grisly evidence to which you refer. The law tends to reserve capital punishment for the extraordinary case, and officials actually execute far fewer than they might under such high standards. States execute only a few dozen under the death sentence every year, when thousands of inmates wait on death row, many of them dying natural deaths after years or even decades under the death sentence.

The death penalty remains controversial for several reasons including the long death-row waits. Statistical studies show that courts apply it unevenly from case to case. Very similar cases produce opposite results, the death penalty in one and no death penalty in the other, making its application appear arbitrary and capricious. Worse, studies show its discriminatory application relative to the race of the convicted person. Non-majority defendants suffer it more frequently than majority defendants (African Americans more frequently than Caucasian Americans). The manner of execution can also create controversy, particularly when the inmate does not die swiftly and relatively painlessly. States execute either by lethal injection or electrocution, some having switched from one to the other in attempts to ensure that the manner of execution is not unconstitutionally cruel and unusual punishment.

The most controversial aspect of the death penalty though may simply be its profound nature that does not allow for repentance, rehabilitation, and redemption. The death penalty is a one-way street. Eye-for-an-eye justice may sound simple, balanced, and attractive, but even in Old Testament times judges ameliorated its obvious harshness to accomplish redemptive ends. Murder is a one-way act. The victim has no hope of return. Yet *two* deaths do not necessarily set *one* death aright. The law will undoubtedly long continue to work out these profoundly difficult and important questions.

53

Living Vicariously

Question

An employee of mine did something stupid that got a customer hurt. Now I've got a letter from the customer's lawyer telling *me* to pay up. I didn't tell my employee to do anything stupid. What law says that I have to pay for another's wrong?

Answer

The law calls paying for another's wrong *vicarious liability*. Instead of *living* vicariously, you *pay* vicariously.

Like so many concepts in the law, vicarious liability can sound unfair at first blush but actually makes good sense. The unfairness has exactly to do with how you put it: you didn't hire an employee to do something wrong. You may have even had work training not to do what this employee did and work rules against it. When it comes to employees, though, your effort to prevent wrongs may not matter. You, the employer, may still be liable. The theory of employer vicarious liability is that your enterprise should bear responsibility for the careless harms that it causes when employees cause those harms. Enterprises carry out their mission through their employees. Financially responsible enterprises insure against careless losses that employees cause in the course of their employment.

Vicarious liability does not mean that you pay for every employee wrong. The wrong must occur in the course of employment. If the employee hurts someone at home while off duty, then the employer does not pay. The employment relationship alone is not enough for vicarious liability. The harm must also occur during the course of the employment. If the employee hurts someone while on some personal frolic from work, then the employer does not pay. Playing flag football on a lunch break or coming back from lunch drunk and getting in a fight would be likely examples of personal frolics for which the employer would ordinarily have no vicarious liability. The line between work and play can get blurred, but vicarious liability requires courts to draw that line.

Also, in most cases, if the employee hurts someone *intentionally* while at work, then the employer ordinarily does not pay. Vicarious liability usually applies only to negligent rather than purposeful harms, unless the employer expects the employee to take deliberate actions. If an employee brings a gun to work to shoot a customer, then the employer would ordinarily not pay for the deliberate harm. Yet if the employer hires a security guard to eject unruly customers, and the guard overzealously injures one such customer, then the employer may have vicarious liability.

Employer liability is not the only kind of vicarious liability. While the laws vary some from state to state, many states impose vicarious liability when an owner of a vehicle or other dangerous instrument consents to its use by another. The owner may have to pay when the user harms others. States also impose vicarious liability for partners and other joint venturers. If one partner injures someone in the partnership's course, then the other partner may have to pay for the injury. States also impose vicarious liability when one person owes a common duty with another. A landlord, for instance, may have to pay for a tenant's harm caused

151

by the negligence of the management company the landlord hired. Just because you hire someone to do what you are supposed to do does not mean that you have no responsibility for doing it.

Akin to vicarious liability are claims for direct liability for negligent hiring, retention, and supervision. Say that you decide to take a large tree down in your home's side yard. If you hire a competent tree company to remove it but the company damages your neighbor's residence in doing so, you may not have any liability. On the other hand, if you hire a fly-by-night contractor you knew or should have known did not have the equipment or skills to remove the tree, or you supervise the contractor's work carelessly, causing your neighbor damage, then you would likely have direct negligence liability for your own fault in bringing about the harm.

The moral is to be careful in what you do, careful in whom you hire, and well insured whenever doing work likely to cause injury. Liability insurance generally applies to both direct and vicarious liability. From what you say, you may or may not have to pay, depending on what stupid thing your employee did and when your employee did it. Get the demand letter to your liability insurer, or if you have none, then to your lawyer.

52

Being Careful Whom You Trust

Question

My neighbor borrowed my pickup truck for a load of bark. His 17-year-old son then wrecked it running a stop sign and T-boning a van full of kids. Now the kids' lawyer is threatening to take everything I own. I didn't run any stop signs. Can they hold me liable?

Answer

Probably, yes. While state laws on the subject vary, many states recognize vehicle-owner liability whenever the negligent driver uses the vehicle with the owner's consent.

Vehicle-owner liability makes sense in these situations. Vehicle owners have more control than anyone else over who gets to use their vehicle. If you place your vehicle in the hands of an unlicensed, drunken driver, then shame on you. You should pay for any harm that befalls. Some states have owner-responsibility statutes that make the vehicle owners liable for injuries caused by consensual use. Some of those statutes presume consent whenever a family member of the owner drives the vehicle. Hide the keys. If your teenage child drives your vehicle, then you are liable for any resultant harm. Other states follow common-law rules holding owners liable for harm attendant on consensual use. The point is that vehicles present dangers especially when in the hands of irresponsible drivers. Owners generally pay because they are the least-cost risk avoiders.

Vehicle owners are also supposed to be financially responsible for harm caused by their vehicles. State laws require that owner-registrants insure their motor vehicles when operated on the public highway. Violation of those mandatory-insurance laws can result in fines, incarceration, and suspension of driving privileges, depending on the state's law. While substantial percentages of vehicle owners ignore the mandatory liability insurance laws (up to 20% or more in some states), most vehicles are insured. Liability insurance has the purpose and effect of spreading the loss of any one person who suffers serious injury in a motor-vehicle accident. Vehicle owners usually do not pay for the loss or even to defend the claim. Their insurers pay for the loss and for defense of the claim.

Not every vehicle use is consensual. If someone were to steal your vehicle, then you would not likely be liable for any harm that they caused. Their use would not be consensual. The cases of non-consensual use get a little harder when the user is an underage child of the vehicle's owner, taking the vehicle for a joy ride. Some states have extended the owner's insurance coverage to the joy-riding minor, while other states have not. Your example actually indicates another gray area of the law. If you permit a friend to use your vehicle, then are you permitting your friend to loan your vehicle to the friend's teenager or some other user? Courts sometimes extend the owner's vicarious liability to a second user as long as the owner did not expressly restrict use to the first user, and the first user consented to the second user's use.

In the end, though, you have a few ways of controlling this careless-other-driver risk. One is not to let others use your vehicle. If you are the only who uses it, then you pay only for your own negligence. Another way is to loan your vehicle only to careful drivers. Even though it might be hard for you to know who is careful and who is not, you could at least keep it out of the hands of inexperienced teenage drivers. Perhaps the best way to limit your risk though is to be sure that you carry sufficiently high insurance policy limits on your vehicle. Insurers insure only up to agreed-upon limits. Depending on state law, those limits can be as low as $10,000 or $20,000. You may have insured for more, say, $50,000, $100,000, or $300,000. Increasing your insurance limits to $500,000 or $1,000,000 is often not that expensive relative to the rest of your motor-vehicle-insurance premium.

One final tip: don't put your name on the title of your teenage child's first vehicle or even on your spouse's vehicle. Wherever you indicate formal ownership, you may be creating vicarious liability for the driver's negligent harms. Title vehicles in the name of the most-common driver only, whenever possible. And insure, insure, insure. Driving vehicles is by far the most dangerous thing that most of us do.

51

A World of Hurt

Question

I ran a little business on my own for years before recently hiring my first couple of employees. My payroll company had me pay what it called *comp insurance*. Then one of my employees hurt his back at work, and my comp rates went through the roof. What's the deal?

Answer

Your comp rates may feel like a raw deal to you, but worker injuries are a cost of doing business. Keep a safe workplace, find work for your injured employees where you can, and shop for better rates.

State worker's compensation laws require employers to guarantee compensation for workplace injuries. When an employee suffers unintentional injury in the course of employment, the employer or its worker's compensation insurer pays for reasonably necessary medical expense and a substantial percentage of the employee's wage loss. Worker's compensation is a no-fault system. Injured employees receive benefits whether or not they or the employer were at fault. The good news for you is that in tradeoff, employees may not sue the employer or co-workers for negligence to recover other losses that fall outside the limited statutory benefits. In some cases, comp benefits cost a lot less than the employer would have paid in a negligence lawsuit.

That does not mean that comp insurance is cheap. Often, it is not. As you now know, your payroll company did the right thing by having you purchase comp insurance. Employers must insure for or otherwise guarantee worker's compensation benefits. Comp insurance is highly ratable, meaning that you pay more when your industry is more dangerous or your specific workplace has a poor record of injuries and comp claims. Comp insurance is often a costly business expense depending on injury and claim rates. High comp rates is one reason why employers adopt aggressive safety programs. Reducing workplace injuries is a good place to start. Shopping around for lower rates may also be an alternative to paying the higher rates. High comp rates affect businesses. State legislatures frequently modify comp legislation to control or influence insurance rates.

To further control comp costs, don't pay benefits that you need not pay. Comp laws do have some disqualifying circumstances. Depending on the applicable law and the injury circumstances, employees may not receive benefits if they intended their own injury or their actions were due to their own drunkenness or other misconduct unrelated to work. Moreover, to qualify for comp benefits, the employee must ordinarily be able to attribute the injury to a specific traumatic workplace event. If your employee's bad back had been just a chronically bad back with no particular workplace injury, then you would not have paid. Worker's compensation does not ordinarily pay for chronic degenerative conditions, although comp will often cover certain occupational diseases.

Just because an employee claims benefits does not mean that you or your insurer must pay. If you have evidence that the injury was not work-related or that your employee is more able to

157

work than the employee claims, then notify your insurer of your concern. Comp insurers retain counsel to investigate and challenge false or exaggerated claims. When disputes over comp claims arise, they go before administrative tribunals rather than general-jurisdiction courts. Don't take the dispute into your own hand though by firing the injured employee. Employers must not retaliate against employees who seek worker's compensation benefits.

So again, your high comp rates may look like a bad deal to you, but the comp benefits may be a godsend to your injured employee. And they are a cost of doing business. Manage the costs, but respect the benefits.

50

The Tax Man Cometh

Question

I just heard about this guy who never filed his taxes. After a decade of cheating the government, things may have finally caught up with him. What can the government do to tax cheats?

Answer

Anything it wants. Well, not quite, but to the obstinate non-filer it might soon seem that way.

Tax authorities, whether state or federal, rely primarily on voluntary compliance. Any democratic republic must rely to a great extent on the virtue of its citizenry. Unless the vast majority of citizens are basically decent and law abiding, all hope for liberty, order, and prosperity is lost. This principle applies equally or especially to taxation. Tax authorities would have little hope of chasing down every tax cheater unless the vast majority of us recognize tax obligations as valid and pay our taxes voluntarily. As in every other regulatory subject, government would simply lack the enforcement resources if we all decided to break the law at once.

159

That said, tax authorities do some things to influence and increase voluntary compliance. Foremost, employers withhold income taxes, paying those taxes directly to the government. The non-filer about whom you heard may in this way actually have paid most or all of his taxes through employer withholding. He might even have gotten over payments back from the government, if he had filed annual tax returns as the law requires. Employers also issue W-2 forms, while other payors issue 1099 forms, reporting to you and disclosing to tax authorities monies that you receive on which you may owe taxes. These disclosures give the federal Internal Revenue Service and state tax authorities a leg up on identifying tax cheaters. They also encourage voluntary compliance. Some taxpayers are more willing to comply if they know the government is watching.

Another way that tax authorities increase voluntary compliance is to make a deterrent example of those who do not comply. The Internal Revenue Service has substantial enforcement powers. It employs thousands of auditors and enforcement agents to investigate, discover, and determine tax liabilities. Failure to follow the tax laws can certainly result in civil proceedings leading to regulatory determinations for back taxes, penalties, and interest. The IRS can place liens on real and personal property and accounts to force unwilling obligors to make due and owing tax payments. Try selling your home with a tax lien on it. The tax authorities will get their fair share of the proceeds. Civil enforcement is frequent and effective. The IRS even maintains programs encouraging others to report suspected taxpayer abuses of the tax laws.

The penalties increase when taxpayers deliberately violate the tax law, knowing that they are cheating the government through false filings. Tax fraud is federal and state crime. The IRS can prosecute dishonest taxpayers, pursuing and proving charges of federal tax crimes. The IRS employs agents with special forensic skills including the ability to locate and recover electronic records. The criminal sanctions for tax fraud can include not only fines but incarceration. The IRS advertises one of the highest conviction rates in federal enforcement. Tax defrauders go to prison, sometimes for long times. Federal prison can be a very stiff deterrent for tax cheats.

The person you mentioned who never files his tax returns will likely face penalties even if he didn't owe any taxes because of taxes his employer withheld. The IRS assesses failure-to-file penalties that can be steeper than the failure-to-pay penalties. Tax returns are the way that you and the IRS keep straight on how much you owe or should get back from the government. Good cause for failing to file may excuse some or all of the penalties but not willful neglect. Stay on top of your taxes. File on time, or request and comply with filing extensions. Don't be a tax cheat. Crime does not pay.

49

Pay to Play

Question

A young driver paying too much attention to her cell phone drove her vehicle right into the rear of my vehicle the other day, causing a couple thousand dollars in damage. Then I found out that she was uninsured. Doesn't the law require drivers to insure their vehicles?

Answer

State laws require vehicle owners and registrants to insure their vehicles, not necessarily vehicle drivers.

You can generally drive another's vehicle without yourself being insured. Lots of drivers hold driver's licenses without owning a vehicle. They do not generally have to purchase insurance to drive someone else's vehicle. Owners and registrants though must insure motor vehicles when operated on the public highways. State insurance codes generally require the insurance for those vehicles. As an administrative-enforcement mechanism, state vehicle codes generally require proof of insurance to register the vehicle and to get the license plate or updated tags. Without the proof of insurance, you don't get the plate or tags. A vehicle owner must pay to play. Operating a vehicle on the public highways is a privilege, and not a free one at that.

Despite these laws and administrative mechanisms, lots of vehicle owners allow their uninsured vehicles onto the public highways. Statistics show uninsured-vehicle rates varying from state to state. The historically highest rates have been in Mississippi and California at around 25%. That figure means that one out of every four vehicles in those states does not have the required insurance. To put it another way, all other things being equal, you stand around a one-out-of-four chance of the vehicle that hits you being uninsured. Other states like Vermont have historically low uninsured-vehicle rates, as low as around 5%, meaning that only 1 out of 20 vehicles is uninsured in those states.

High uninsured-vehicle rates suggest that owners find ways to get around proof-of-insurance and other administrative requirements meant to keep vehicles insured. One way they do so is to pay the premium for only the first month, submit the proof of insurance for the plate or tags, and then let the policy lapse. Some insurers will even sell a policy and provide the proof for just one *week* of insurance, making it even cheaper to drive uninsured for the rest of the year until the owner needs updated tags. Some states require vehicle insurers to notify the state when a policy lapses, giving law-enforcement officials a chance to put a boot on the uninsured vehicle or otherwise attempt to keep it off the road.

States also punish those who own and operate uninsured vehicles. While the tags may be up to date, when an officer pulls a vehicle over for a moving violation and the owner cannot produce valid proof of insurance, the owner gets a citation or charge. In some states, the citation may cost as much as a few hundred dollars. Some states also provide for incarcerating the guilty vehicle owner, although that punishment is likely rare. No matter how hard state legislatures, law-enforcement officials, and judges try, it appears to be very difficult to keep uninsured vehicles off the road. Policy concerns can weigh in the opposite direction. A family needs a breadwinner in order to eat, and breadwinners often require private transportation. Modest enforcement levels may be tacit recognition of other higher-priority concerns.

Incidentally, just because the person who hit your vehicle was uninsured may not mean that you get no help with your vehicle's repair. Several states are no-fault states where you must insure your own vehicle for repair. Insurers call it *collision coverage*. State law generally does not require that you buy collision coverage, but many of us do. So notify your own motor-vehicle insurer. Also, the unlawfully uninsured remain personally liable. While collecting on a judgment against an uninsured vehicle owner may be difficulty, it may not be impossible. Consider pursuing the other driver and vehicle owner in small-claims court. And always pay to play. The law requires it, and it will preserve your rights.

48

The Seven-Year Ditch

Question

My finances look like I am headed for bankruptcy, even though I make a good living. That's not so bad, is it? I figured that with my good income, I would just start over with a new house, new car, and anything else that I need or want on credit.

Answer

If it sounds too good to be true, then it usually isn't true. While bankruptcy can discharge your debts, creditors can and will use your bankruptcy to deny you credit or to charge you more.

As soon as you file for bankruptcy, the bankruptcy code protects you from creditor actions to collect your old debts. The bankruptcy court stays collection actions. In Chapter 7 cases, if you complete the bankruptcy filing meeting all requirements of the court and code, then the court will issue an order for discharge, meaning that you need no longer pay the discharged debts. In Chapter 13 wage-earner bankruptcy, you would ordinarily pay a portion of old debts that the bankruptcy court consolidates, until you complete the plan after three to five years, effectively discharging any remaining old debt. Creditors whose debts the court discharged must not take any action to collect those discharged debts. Doing so would be a violation of federal law and could constitute contempt of the bankruptcy court's discharge order. Bankruptcy discharge puts you in the driver's seat as to old debt.

Bankruptcy though does not put you in the driver's seat as to new credit. Creditors are not dummies. Just because you wipe them out in bankruptcy does not mean that they will come rushing back to you loan you money again. To the contrary, your bankruptcy goes on your credit record for seven years in the case of a Chapter 13 filing and ten years in the case of a Chapter 7 filing. Bankruptcy reduces your credit score significantly, likely putting a home mortgage and other credit well beyond your reach. You will likely not be able to get credit at all for some things you once did. When you do find that you qualify for credit, that credit is likely to be significantly more expensive in terms of interest rate and fees than it would have been without the bankruptcy. Creditors may also require security or guarantors.

Of course, placing credit beyond the reach of a bankrupt is not necessarily a bad thing. You should also ask yourself why you are in such a hurry to borrow money again when owing debt got you into bankruptcy in the first place. Bankruptcy does little to no good unless you first control the spending or other habits and manage the circumstances that created the unmanageable debt that drove you to bankruptcy. You can file for bankruptcy again, although you cannot receive a second discharge within eight years of your first discharge (assuming both are under Chapter 7; you may be able to obtain a Chapter 13 bankruptcy as soon as within four years of a Chapter 7 discharge). But no one should plan to do so. You should plan for the opposite, never to file for bankruptcy again. Bankruptcy is not a pleasant experience. Debtors can feel substantial shame, worthlessness, depression, and embarrassment.

166

So get on a budget. Because you have a good income, you should probably not be having financial problems. Something is wrong, and a budget will tell you what. Get financial help from someone close to you who knows how to manage money. Get your financial house in order before thinking about bankruptcy. Who knows? You may be able to avoid bankruptcy entirely with a good bit of the right help. If you must file, then expect not to have available credit for a long time, as much as seven years. Prepare to manage your finances without incurring substantial loan obligations, which after all, may be a wise course in any case.

47

Fit to Be Tied

Question

We had the strangest thing happen the other evening at our neighborhood association's annual meeting. We took three votes on different subjects, and they all ended up in ties. We worked it out, but what does the law say in the case of a tie election?

Answer

Depends on the election.

We hold a lot of elections in America, so tie votes may not be as rare as they might seem. We have political elections and not just major ones for national or statewide offices but local elections for everything from mayor, councilmember, judge, prosecutor, drain commissioner, and the proverbial dog-catcher. We also have referenda deciding issues like tax levies, bond authorizations, and social initiatives. We have corporate elections for for-profit and non-profit boards, and board votes for officers, policies, mergers, and acquisitions. We vote within unions and sometimes within workplaces especially on committees. We vote within schools and parent-teacher organizations, and in condominium associations and neighborhoods—as in your case. With all of these elections, we should have more tie votes than we do.

Different state and federal laws and constitutions make different provisions for tie elections of different kinds. In some cases, the law has another person cast a tie-breaking vote or another body vote to break the tie. For example, under the U.S. Constitution, the U.S. Senate breaks ties by vote of the Vice President of the United States, who serves as the President of the Senate. For another example, under the U.S. Constitution, the U.S. House of Representatives breaks tie votes of the Electoral College for U.S. President. The nation actually had a tie vote in the Electoral College in 1800, when Thomas Jefferson and his running mate Aaron Burr tied because of an anomaly in the voting process since corrected. The House broke the tie in favor of Jefferson. The House elected the President a second time in 1824 not because of a tie but because no candidate won a majority in the Electoral College. Interestingly, the House breaks Electoral College ties by state-by-state voting delegations with only one equal vote per state.

In other cases, the law would break the tie by chance, such as by the flip of a coin, putting candidate names in a hat, or drawing lots. As many as 35 states have laws authorizing tie-breakers by chance. Some of those state provisions specify the form of chance, while others leave the form to the election officials. Does drawing names from a hat seem a little less arbitrary than flipping a coin? In still other cases, the law holds the tie election invalid, requiring a new election, usually within a short period of a couple or few weeks. Hope that someone changes his or her mind. The reason given for a new election is that the law should not disenfranchise voters through forms of chance. Elections are not supposed to be a literal roll of the dice.

Because of the smaller number of voting shareholders or board members, corporate ties may be the most common. Candidates who tie in private settings may more easily resolve the situation by one candidate withdrawing, as often happens. Better that one withdraw than the election divide and damage the corporation. State corporation laws may also provide that if shareholders deadlock on electing new board members, then the current board members continue serving. Those laws may also give the corporation or its officers, directors, or shareholders the right to seek a court's relief to break deadlocks, either by appointing a tie-breaking board member, removing one or more of the deadlocked board members, or even dissolving the corporation.

For other private bodies where no law dictates how to break a tie vote, consider Roberts Rules of Order, which indicates to keep repeating the vote until it no longer produces a tie. Once again, hope someone changes their mind. And then we have recounts, a right granted by law or custom in many jurisdictions, as to political elections. When a candidate demands a recount of a tie vote, the recount may correct the count and break the tie. On the other hand, when a candidate demands a recount of a close vote, the recount may correct the count to create a tie. Perhaps if tie votes and near-tie votes teach us anything, it is how strange it is that we credit and trust bare majorities. To the winner, one vote more than the loser is always a mandate.

46

Jack of All Trades

Question

Some of you lawyers seem to know a lot about a lot of things, but the other day I asked another lawyer friend a simple legal question, and she said she had no idea because she was only a benefits lawyer. Do you all specialize these days?

Answer

No. A lot of us specialize, but a lot of us don't. Some of us are proverbial jacks of all trades while masters of, well, some.

Licensed lawyers have passed a comprehensive bar exam, meaning that at one time they had a lot of law knowledge about a lot of subjects. Law schools vary, but most offer broad curricula covering literally dozens of law subjects. A new lawyer will know a lot about a lot of legal things. Experienced lawyers on the other hand may not. Use it or lose it. As years go by, lawyers tend to learn much more about the area or areas in which they practice while forgetting more about the areas in which they don't. You do find experienced lawyers who know a lot about only one subject area or very few subject areas—only the ones in which they practice.

Your benefits-lawyer friend is a good example. Employment law is a complex specialty. Federal, state, and local governments enact dozens of employment laws, while administrative agencies like OSHA, the IRS, the National Labor Relations Board, and the Department of Labor enact dozens more employment- and labor-law regulations. The specialty of employment law has several subspecialties like labor law (the law of unions), employment rights and litigation, worker's compensation, and employee-benefits law. Each of those subspecialties is large, complex, and unique enough for lawyers to practice either only or primarily in that one area. Your friend is not alone. The law profession has many other benefits lawyers, just as it has labor lawyers, worker's comp lawyers, and so on.

Specializing enables a lawyer to hone the lawyer's peculiar craft. The specialist lawyer can often be much more efficient at whatever service the lawyer provides in the specialty than a general-practice lawyer would be providing the same specialty service. You get quick and good at what you do when you do a lot of it and little else. That efficiency is one reason that large firms can have advantages in certain fields over small firms. In a large firm, you may find multiple practice groups, say, one for employment law, another for mergers and acquisitions, another for insurance defense, and so on. Within each of those practice groups, you may find lawyers specializing in subspecialties within those practice areas. For example, the insurance-defense group may have lawyers specializing in personal-injury defense, products-liability defense, malpractice defense, and so on.

Lawyers in small firms do not always have that luxury. They cannot pass a complex matter in a peculiar law field to an experienced specialist down the hall in the same firm. Lawyers in small firms tend instead to either maintain a general practice in which they do many things well or to develop a boutique practice in which they specialize, referring clients with other matters to other firms. The general practitioners know what matters they can handle competently and what matters they cannot. They may represent personal-injury claimants, defend persons charged with crimes, and help incorporate new small businesses. Yet they may refer out complex medical-malpractice cases, murder cases, and mergers and acquisition work even though each of those special cases is within one of their general fields.

The world needs both specialist lawyers and general-practice lawyers, just as it needs specialist doctors and general-practitioner doctors. Small rural towns need general-practice lawyers, while large metropolitan areas need specialist lawyers. Large corporations need specialist lawyers for their complex matters, but they also need generalist lawyers to act as corporate counsel and trusted advisors. Individual clients need general-practice lawyers to help them with routine consumer matters but may need a specialist lawyer for the rare complex matter, perhaps for a bankruptcy (a common specialty) or to patent an invention (intellectual property being another specialty). When you need a lawyer, consider finding a general practitioner who can either help you with that matter and other future matters, or refer you to specialist lawyers when your matter is too peculiar and complex.

45

Who Gets the Kids?

Question

My nephew and his ex-wife are going into their third year of fighting over who gets the kids. Things were difficult from the moment that they first separated. It has gotten little better since their divorce. Will they have no end to their custody battle?

Answer

Maybe not until the children reach adulthood.

Child custody is the classic divorce battle. Children can become pawns that the parents' emotional wounds manipulate in pitched battle. While both sides will say that the battle is all about the kids, and indeed both mother and father may care deeply about with which parent the children spend the bulk of their time, child custody can carry with it so much more than simply more time with the kids. In emotional terms, the custodial parent can claim victory, vindication, and even vengeance, all of which the wounds of divorce and its causes may make sweeter than the considerable custody-battle costs. The custodial parent also usually wins child support, adding financial gain to the emotional satisfaction of having gained custody after a legal struggle.

Divorce or other family break up should not be that way. If anything, the parents ought to protect the children, to try to make livable for them the difficult process of making two households out of one. Divorces can scar children emotionally just as divorce can scar the spouses. Wiser parents make heroic attempts to keep the children out of it. Sometimes, heroic effort by one parent is unavailing. It only takes one unreasoning litigant to pick a custody fight, particularly when that litigant is an unfit parent. Custody disputes are not always the fault of both parents. They are sometimes the fault and weapon of just one.

State law determines both what constitutes child custody and who gets it. Generally, child custody means that the children reside substantially more of the time with the custodial parent than with the non-custodial parent. In its simplest terms, to reside means to sleep overnight. In shared-custody arrangements, the children may spend about equal time with each parent, but once the time tips substantially in favor of one parent over the other, that parent becomes the custodial parent, reducing the other parent's status to child visitation also known as parenting time. Parenting time is often one mid-week overnight each week plus every other weekend. State law may also divide custody into legal custody and physical custody. Parents will often share joint legal custody, generally meaning the right to make major decisions (schooling, faith instruction, medical care) affecting the child's welfare.

Judges can have a very hard time of it sorting out which of two well-qualified parents makes the slightly better custodial parent. Depending on the state law and procedures, judges may have the help of professional custody investigators, assigned social workers, and family-court referees or magistrates. State law provides the custody standard, typically a best-interest-of-the-child standard. The decision does not depend on which parent needs, wants, or deserves custody more, although to the parents it

175

may seem that way. Rather, the decision depends on which custody arrangement will serve the children better.

State law may require judges and custody investigators to address a statutory list of child-custody factors. Those factors tend to include the relative fitness of each parent, whether either parent subjects the other or the children to mental or physical abuse, with which parent the children have the current established custodial environment, and, if the children are old enough, with which parent the children would prefer to live. Another important factor can be the willingness of the parent to support the other parent's relationship with the children. Children benefit from strong relationships with both parents, even if the parents themselves cannot get along with one another. It does not help a parent's custody case to run the other parent down in front of the children.

The worst custody battles may not end until the order for custody ends. Child-custody orders typically remain in place until the children turn age 18 or graduate from high school, whichever is later (often with an older age limit such as 19 ½ for older children still attending high school). Yet as children mature into their teens and late teens, their physical and emotional independence makes custody orders less significant. Older teens tend to reside where they wish, either with one parent or the other or with neither parent, no matter what their parents and the courts say about their best welfare. Sometimes the only solution to a custody battle is the kids growing up.

44

Whose Domain?

Question

The state wants to take part of my neighbor's land to turn it over to a developer to build a private showplace and casino. They're telling him that they'll pay the fair value of the land, but what if my neighbor doesn't want to sell? The government can't just take it, can they?

Answer

Possibly, yes. The U.S. Constitution permits government to take land for public use as long as the government pays just compensation for it. The law calls that government power the power of *eminent domain*. Sometimes to fulfill its public function, government must take private property for public use. Imagine trying to acquire the land for an airport, freeway extension, or military base, for instance. One holdout landowner could ruin the whole project or, sensing that power, charge the government an exorbitant price for the land. Many public projects might never get built. Eminent domain is a critical government power, although one (your neighbor knows all too well) that the law must carefully circumscribe to avoid government abuse of landowners.

Until recently, public use meant things like public highways, public parks, public arenas, and public hospitals. You get the *public* part of the picture. But recently, the Supreme Court interpreted public *use* expressly to include for some public *purpose* such as for private developers to redevelop blighted urban lands. The Supreme Court majority reasoned that redevelopment, even if by private developers, accomplished the public purposes of creating jobs, increasing tax revenue, and removing urban blight. Under that recent Supreme Court authority, government has the power to take blighted land for fair market value and then turn it over to private developers to remove the blight while creating jobs and generating tax revenues. That power means that the government-taken land does not necessarily end up for public *use*, as the courts had previously construed the Constitution to require, but nonetheless for a public *purpose*.

As you might imagine, the Supreme Court's decision arguably extending the government's power of eminent domain did not sit too well with many landowners. State constitutions and laws can further limit state and local eminent-domain powers. Just because the U.S. Constitution permits it does not mean that the state must also permit it. Some states had already limited eminent domain explicitly for public uses, not simply public purposes. After the Supreme Court's decision, many more states limited eminent domain, rejecting its use purely for economic redevelopment. Those changes have in effect diminished the impact of the Supreme Court's unpopular decision.

Your description of your neighbor's situation does not mention any public purpose that the state is pursuing by turning your neighbor's property over to a developer for a showplace and casino. You did not say that your neighbor's property is blighted, that the property is in a depressed area needing economic revitalization, or anything of the sort. The state may or may not have a public purpose behind its attempted taking. Even if the state did have a public purpose, a private showplace and casino is very likely not a public use, and your state's law may further restrict the state's eminent-domain powers to public uses rather than merely public purposes.

Your neighbor should be working with a lawyer who has expertise in eminent-domain matters if your neighbor doesn't want to sell. The lawyer may be able to prove that the state has no public purpose behind the taking or may find further limitations in the state law and constitution. Failing that, the lawyer may help your neighbor get higher value for the taken property. Sometimes, a man's castle is his home only as long as the government does not have a public use for it.

43

Water, Water, Everywhere

Question

I was preparing to do a little grading in the back of my suburban property so that my wife could enlarge her vegetable garden, when the state's department of environmental quality posted a stop-work order on my door. The order said something about "wetlands" even though we've never seen any water back there, just a few cattails. The state can't stop me, can it?

Answer

Yes. State legislatures have determined that wetlands are important to an area's ecology, passing environmental codes that preserve and protect them. Administrative agencies like state departments of environmental quality enforce those legislative codes. A stop-work order means what it says. If you continue to affect the putative wetland area, then you may face the administrative fines, contempt of court, or other sanctions.

The public has taken some time to understand the value of wetlands. Their value is not simply that they look aesthetically pleasing to some or that they support waterfowl or other marsh game. Wetlands serve a complex function in the ecosystem that includes preserving and improving water quality. Rains have to go someplace. When rains percolate through soil, particularly wetlands soil, the soil captures particulate matter of all sorts, whether waste, bacteria, or other materials that pollute the water, thus serving a cleansing purpose. If instead rainwater simply runs off land directly into rivers, lakes, and other bodies of water, then the surface water has not had the benefit of cleansing percolation. Storm-water runoff can cause other harms and hazards like soil erosion. Wetlands mitigate these hazards.

You can appreciate the value of wetlands by examining the nearest shopping mall. In all likelihood, artificial water-retention areas ring the mall's vast non-permeable surfaces. Buildings and parking lots do not percolate water. Vast quantities of storm water can run off of large buildings and parking areas. That water has to go somewhere. When it runs straight into storm sewers, it may go straight from there into rivers or lakes. Water-retention ponds reduce storm-water runoff, preserving and improving the quality of water from which a municipality may draw its drinking and other service water. Natural wetlands serve the same function. If everyone in your suburb filled over the large and small wetlands on their properties, then your suburb would be contributing more pollutants to the areas larger bodies of water, making cleansing that water for human use more difficult and expensive.

You don't need to see water for a wetland. State laws define wetlands as much by vegetation and animal life as by the presence of surface water. You may not see the water, but if enough is there to support wetland vegetation or aquatic life like certain frogs and turtles, then you've got wetlands. Cattails and other marsh species are telltale wetlands signs. Yet just because you have a wetland on your property does not mean that you cannot use that portion of your property. You may be able to get a permit that will allow you to change the wetland for other uses but to mitigate the damaging environmental effect by creating other wetland areas. You know that pond your spouse always wanted? Maybe it's time your spouse got his or her wish.

Environmental legislation can be controversial because of its direct control of traditional and unusual land uses. Environmental regulators sometimes go too far. Administrative procedures and court access are available to protect your property rights. Consult with a lawyer who has environmental-law expertise about your rights. But don't mess with the state DEQ. Play it by the book.

42

Workin' Overtime

Question

I had been paid overtime at my plant for years until management gave me a new title and salary that about equals my prior hourly wage. Now, no matter how many hours I work each week, my pay stays the same. I'd rather have the overtime. What happened?

Answer

You are right to take a close look at what happened. Classification of employees as exempt or non-exempt from the overtime laws is a big issue. Classification means more than looking at your title and whether you are hourly or salaried. It involves looking at what you actually do for your employer. If all it took to avoid overtime-wage laws was a fancy title and small salary, then you would see a lot more fancy titles and small salaries. Federal and state authorities have pursued enforcement initiatives to catch and correct employers who manipulate the overtime laws to deprive non-exempt employees of due overtime.

Consult a lawyer who has expertise in the overtime laws about your situation because you might deserve the overtime pay.

Both the federal Fair Labor Standards Act and similar state laws require employers to pay non-exempt employees time and a half (150% of the hourly wage) for hours worked over 40 hours in each workweek. Everyone knows that basic time-and-a-half-over-40 rule. The 40-hour workweek has long been a foundation for the American worker and the opportunity to earn more for more than 40 hours important to self-advancement and the achievement of financial and finance-related goals. Many employees depend on receiving overtime pay to make their hourly wage a livable wage. While some employees grumble about overtime, which can seriously interfere with family responsibilities, recreation, and even physical and mental health, many other employees desire overtime for the financial reward it brings.

The key in your situation, like for many other employees, is to determine whether your position is exempt from overtime laws or instead non-exempt and subject to those laws. In policy terms, management does not get overtime. Managers receive different rewards, perhaps bonuses, promotions, or equity in the business, when they work beyond the bedrock 40-hour week. Laborers, who may lack those same opportunities, instead have the advantage of the overtime laws. To be an exempt manager, an employee must first be salaried rather than hourly. Yet changing your pay to salaried rather than hourly is not enough. To be exempt from overtime laws, an employee must also generally be an executive employee, meaning one who supervises two or more other employees, or an administrative employee, meaning one who exercises significant discretion. (Professional and outside sales employees are also exempt.) So unless your employer gave you supervisory duties or administrative discretion along with your new salary, you may still be a non-exempt employee due overtime.

As indicated above, the overtime-wage laws often have strong federal or state administrative enforcement. You may be able to

184

recover not only the lost overtime pay but also a doubling of the unpaid amount or other statutory damages, costs, and fees. You may not need the help of a private lawyer, if the applicable federal or state agency has the resources to investigate and pursue your matter, and the interest in doing so. You might still consider a private lawyer's review either to identify the applicable agency to which to refer your matter or to ensure that you are pursuing all of your wage and employment rights. For instance, when calculating the time-and-a-half amount for overtime, your employer should have been including regular bonuses and the monetary value of any employer-provided meals or lodging.

Oh, and one last thing. While you always want good relationship with your employer, and few of us really want to think or claim that our employer is breaking the law, your employer should not be retaliating against you if you ask for a lawyer's or agency's help in determining your wage-law rights. Check the issue out with a lawyer's help. An employee deserves a lawful wage.

41

How Little Is Enough?

Question

I've been hearing a lot about raising the minimum wage. I can see that doing so could help many working adults, particularly those in single-parent households who have no other source of income than their minimum-wage job. But kids are hardly working these days, and increasing the minimum wage is going to make it even harder for them to get a job. What's the right approach?

Answer

You hit the question on the head. Minimum-wage laws involve matters of both law and policy. Let's consider the law first.

Federal and state laws each set minimum hourly wages for employees. You can pay a contractor as much or as little as you can bargain for in the price. If the contractor barely makes anything or even loses money on your job, then that is the contractor's tough luck. Business owners sometimes make money and sometimes lose money. Plenty of business owners end up

186

working for less than the minimum wage when the business goes south. With employees, it's different. If you have an employee, then you must pay the employee the higher of the federal or state minimum hourly wage unless the employee's position is exempt from the minimum-wage laws. An hourly wage is one that varies with the number of hours the employee works in a week. If you fail to pay the minimum wage, then your employee may sue you, gain the amount you should have paid, and have that amount doubled or otherwise increased by statutory damages, interest, costs, and fees. Pay the minimum wage. The alternative is more risky and expensive. Private lawyers take these cases, while affected employees also often find administrative enforcement available.

Minimum-wage laws apply to workers whom their employer pays by the hour. Federal minimum-wage law exempts salaried employees who are executive (supervisory), administrative (exercising discretion), professional, and outside-sales employees. Yet paying one of these exempt employees a fixed salary that does not vary with the number of hours worked, rather than an hourly rate, does not really get around the minimum-wage laws. Federal law permits federal agency regulations to set a minimum salary that ensures that in most cases the salaried worker will earn at least the minimum hourly wage. The current minimum salary is $455 per week, which for a 40-hour week would work out to a little more than $11 per hour. You can see that if the salaried worker works 50, 60, or more hours in a week at the minimum salary, then the worker may earn under the federal or state minimum hourly wage.

The current federal hourly minimum wage is $7.25. The federal rate sets the floor, but many states have higher rates than the federal rate, as high as $9 per hour or slightly more. Some cities also have minimum-wage laws raising the rate even higher than the federal and state rates to $10 per hour or more. The policy justifications for a higher minimum wage begin with providing a sustainable wage particularly for single-income households. Many minimum-wage earners work in multiple-income households so that the minimum wage is simply supplementing a higher-than-minimum-wage income earned by someone else in the household, perhaps a parent or spouse. Yet many minimum-wage earners provide the only earned income in a household. Living on one person's minimum wage is difficult to impossible, particularly when the household has multiple members. Increasing the minimum wage can provide a direct benefit to those households.

Yet you are also correct that raising the minimum wage can reduce available employment, particularly for the young and others who lack job experience and skills. You get less of anything that you make more expensive. Raising the minimum wage has at least some effect on employers' willingness to hire low-skill workers. And minimum-wage jobs often provide a critical first step toward higher-wage jobs for the worker who lacks job experience or skills. The net effect of raising the minimum wage can be to help some minimum-wage earners while hurting others who would lose their job or opportunity for a job.

With the federal minimum wage at $7.25 and many states higher (some significantly higher), labor economists should be able to measure the varied effects of minimum-wage differences to inform legislators at the national, state, and local levels. American federalism is one grand, longstanding, and richly successful experiment in governance. Issues like the minimum wage demonstrate just how effective American law and governance can be to respond appropriately to the best interests of all of the nation's citizens. Join the debate over the minimum wage and other important national and local issues.

40

I've Got to Be Me,
What Else Can I See?

Question

We've got a homeowner in our town who puts out signs in his yard for everything. Some are funny, some are political, and some are just plain stupid. The guy's got to be crazy, but then it's his home. Recently, though, city officials sued him to make him take the signs down. What does the city have to say about it?

Answer

The city has very little to say about the content on the signs but something to say about the signs' size and placement.

The court will follow 1st Amendment case law to determine the extent to which the city may interfere with the homeowner's free expression. The U.S. Constitution's 1st Amendment states that Congress shall make no law establishing religion or prohibiting its free exercise, or abridging free speech, free press, free assembly, or freedom to petition the government. Free-speech rights protect not just your freedom to speak but other forms of communicative expression like things that you write including even the signs in the homeowner's yard. The nation's founders saw that government should not tell us what to say or stop us from saying what we think best.

While strictly speaking, the 1st Amendment only states that *Congress* shall make no law abridging free speech, the Supreme Court has held that the 14th Amendment's prohibition on state interference with due process rights means that state and local governments must not interfere with free speech. The 1st Amendment applies to state and local action, not just congressional action. States laws and constitutions may restrict government further. The homeowner in your town has 1st Amendment free-speech rights to protect against unconstitutional city action, particularly if the city bases its action on the content of any of the signs rather than on the signs in general. The courts give content-based restrictions greater scrutiny than content-neutral restrictions. They also give greater scrutiny to non-commercial speech than to commercial speech, such as if the homeowner were advertising a business.

Free-speech rights, though, are not absolute. Government may restrict certain forms of speech based on its harmful nature, like defamatory statements, threats of immediate physical harm, and fraudulent false speech. If the homeowner's signs defamed a local person or business, urged citizens to shoot the mayor, or promoted a fraudulent scheme, then public or private actions in the courts could result in orders to take the signs down. Government may restrict speech that creates a clear and present danger of imminent lawless action, such as inciting rioters to looting and violence, or that creates an imminent threat to public safety, such as shouting "fire!" in a crowded theater. Government may also restrict obscene materials, although defining obscenity has proven a continual challenge.

The homeowner's signs probably do not fall into any of these categories. Yet government may also enact reasonable content-neutral regulations for public health, safety, and welfare. You might wonder what interest the city would have in a homeowner's signs, but distracting roadside signs could affect driver safety. Large signs around the home or near the street could interfere with driver sight lines, side-yard access to the rear of the home, or firefighter access around the home. Courts have also upheld regulations based on aesthetics and even ordinances that restrict political campaign signs to the period right around an election.

In the city's lawsuit, the city will have to demonstrate that its efforts to restrict or remove the homeowner's signs fit into one of these exceptions to 1st Amendment free-speech rights. Follow the lawsuit closely. It implicates important rights.

39

Private Places, Straight Laces

Question

My teenager just told me that her school is searching their lockers. I'm kind of ambivalent about it. I know she doesn't have anything in her locker that she shouldn't, and I'm glad for safety reasons that the school is keeping the lockers in mind, but it still seems too much like snooping. Can the school do that?

Answer

On reasonable suspicion, yes. Without it, probably not.

You are right that citizens have privacy rights against government intrusion. If your teenager attends a public school, then the searching of her locker is a government action against which she may have constitutional protection. We find those rights in the U.S. Constitution's 4th Amendment, prohibiting unreasonable searches. The 4th Amendment guarantees "the right of the people to be secure in their persons, houses, papers, and effects, against unreasonable searches and seizures" except by warrant "upon probable cause" supported by oath or affirmation and describing the places for search or persons or things for

192

seizure. The Supreme Court has interpreted the 4th and 14th Amendments to restrict not only federal officials but also state and local officials from engaging in unreasonable searches and seizures.

As with other constitutional rights, the 4th Amendment right against unreasonable searches and seizures is not absolute. First, as indicated above, government officials who have probable cause to search for evidence of crime may obtain a judge's warrant to do so. If school officials had reports or other bases to believe that students were hiding drugs, guns, explosive devices, stolen goods, or other contraband or weapons in their lockers, then they could obtain a warrant to search those lockers. Yet even without probable, the school may have a limited right to search lockers. Schools are special venues facing special security concerns, particularly in light of school shooting incidents. The courts require school officials to balance student privacy rights with the need to maintain safety and order.

The standard under which the Supreme Court has required school officials to balance privacy rights against safety interests is one of reasonable suspicion. The reasonable-suspicion standard gives school officials somewhat greater leeway to search than law-enforcement officials would have under the probable-cause standard. School officials must take a common-sense approach evaluating all of the circumstances and information. Student reports of a concealed gun would clearly be sufficient to search the suspect student's locker. So too might an anonymous report of hidden drugs coupled with the student's reputation among other students as being a drug dealer. But simply smelling the odor of marijuana in a school hallway would likely not be enough to search all the lockers in that hallway. Courts take these matters on a case-by-case basis.

With a compelling interest or special need, a school may also be able to conduct a random search of lockers. For example, significant evidence of widespread drug dealing and drug abuse within a school may provide a compelling interest for a school to conduct random locker searches for drugs. Cases have upheld the school's right to use a drug-sniffing dog around lockers. If the dog alerts to a specific locker, then the school would have reasonable suspicion for its search. School officials can also simply ask the student to consent to search, although consent in these situations can prove coercive, something the courts must judge.

Politely share your concern with school officials. They may be able to explain to you the circumstances behind and scope of the searches. If their explanation does not satisfy you, then consider consulting with a lawyer who knows school and 4th Amendment law. Your responsible interest could be a good lesson for your teenage student.

38

Vampire State

Question

I've got a friend who refused a breathalyzer test when the police arrived at the scene of a motor-vehicle accident in which he was an involved driver. The police followed his ambulance to the hospital where they made him submit to a blood draw from which the prosecution charged him for drunk driving. Can police force you to give up your own blood that way?

Answer

Not ordinarily, unless the police officers have a search warrant. With a search warrant, forced blood draws are lawful.

The U.S. Constitution's 4th Amendment protects citizens from unreasonable searches and seizures. You are right that generally, police officials cannot simply draw the blood of whomever they wish. While you probably think of police searches as looking through personal property like a car, purse, or suitcase, and seizures as the formal arrest of a person, a forced blood draw is also a search and seizure. That is, the 4th Amendment protects against forced medical tests like blood draws. The Supreme Court has held that to conduct a search and seizure that involves a blood draw, police officials must ordinarily obtain a warrant unless they can show some exigent circumstance.

Of course, getting a warrant can take time, when time is exactly what the suspect hopes to buy before having to submit to blood-alcohol testing. The body absorbs alcohol into the blood stream and dissipates it from the blood stream at predictable rates. Once the suspect stops drinking, blood-alcohol levels initially continue to rise for about one hour (depending on whether food is in the stomach) as the alcohol passes into and through the digestive system. Levels then begin to fall steadily. To get a warrant, police officials must attest to a magistrate or judge that they have probable cause to believe that the suspect has committed a crime (the crime of drunk driving). The longer the delay, the lower may be the suspect's blood-alcohol level when finally tested at the hospital. Unless the hospital tested the suspect's blood anyway because of the accident injuries, which the hospital may well have done, the delay in obtaining a warrant could possibly relieve the suspect of some or all criminal responsibility.

Blood-alcohol tests are a relatively reliable way of proving the influence of alcohol. State statutes defining drunk-driving crimes typically refer to blood-alcohol levels, presuming drunkenness or super-drunkenness at various blood-alcohol levels like .08, .10, and .15, .20, or higher. Blood-alcohol levels are not a perfect indication of the actual influence of alcohol. A habituated drinker may "hold" his or her liquor well. Some individuals can appear relatively sober with extraordinarily high blood-alcohol levels in excess of .20 that would make an infrequent drinker feel and appear stone drunk. The statutory levels simply give a relative degree of certainty to what would otherwise be a highly uncertain judgment of how much alcohol is too much alcohol.

Police have different ways, though, of proving drunk driving in addition to using blood-alcohol levels. A suspect's refusal to take a breathalyzer or submit to a blood draw may under state

196

law create a presumption that the suspect knew he or she was drunk. Depending on the state's law, your friend could suffer conviction, fine, and incarceration, and lose his license, simply for refusing the test under these circumstances. Police may also do other roadside sobriety tests, observing the suspect attempt to walk a straight line, bring finger to nose with eyes shut, stand on one foot, or simply focus with the eyes and speak without slurring. Charges and conviction may then depend on the particular state's law, but often, refusing the test results in a worse penalty or sentence than submitting to the test with poor results.

If in this case the police did not get a warrant when they should have, then your friend's lawyer will likely move to bar the test results from evidence and, if successful, move to dismiss the drunk-driving charge. Your friend should not have been drinking and driving, but the law accepts that one must occasionally let the guilty go free when those who investigate the crime violate important constitutional rights. The rights must be meaningful rather than routinely ignored.

37

When Commitment Is a Bad Thing

Question

Our niece away at college apparently attempted suicide. Now they've got her locked up in a special ward away from her studies, friends, and family, even though she committed no crime. Can they do that? They're treating her worse than a criminal.

Answer

Yes, public-health officials can make emergency civil commitments for a short period such as up to 72 hours and then if necessary ask a probate or family court to extend the commitment long enough to ensure that the ward is no danger to herself or others. Your niece should have hearings and legal representation to ensure that her commitment is appropriate, she gets the diagnosis and care she needs, and her commitment lasts no longer than necessary. Her college studies and family-and-friend relationships come after ensuring her safe life.

Civil commitments are not incarceration for crime, although you are correct that they can at times seem that way. Civil commitments occur within a secure facility, meaning locked windows and doors, and sometimes more such as restraints and forced medication. The embarrassment and isolation of civil commitment can be very difficult, even though it is meant to be the opposite, humane. As in anything that we attempt to do, abuses can occur. Think of the movie *One Flew Over the Cuckoos Nest* (while recognizing that it was only a movie). Mistakes and misunderstandings can also occur. Mental-health professionals are not perfect. Predicting when a person might attempt suicide can be difficult. Predicting when a committed patient won't attempt suicide again can likewise be hard.

Civil commitments nonetheless ensure the health and safety of those patient who, whether temporarily or for a longer term, demonstrate that they are unable to care for themselves because of mental or emotional conditions. Mental-health officials may seek civil commitment of the manic, schizophrenic, paranoid, bulimic, demented, or others, when their conditions lead to behaviors that endanger themselves of others. The dangers can include violence toward others, erratic driving, substance abuse, refusal to eat, refusal of self-care, and other actions and perceptions that make it very difficult or impossible for the person to function without institutional care. The institutions are specifically equipped to provide intensive residential care even if against the patient's wishes.

Suicide is an especially serious, prevalent, and frightening risk for the teenager and young adult. Unusual stress, anxiety, depression, substance abuse, physical or mental abuse, isolation, and other undiagnosed and untreated mental-health conditions can cause a previously healthy teenager or young adult to contemplate or attempt suicide. Diagnosis and treatment of the underlying conditions can be swift and effective, when mental-health professionals have the chance. In the best cases, intensive treatment under commitment after an attempted suicide can correct the course of a life.

Due process of law is the constitutional safeguard against an abusive or unnecessary civil commitment. State officials must not deprive a person of liberty without telling them why and giving them an opportunity for a judge to hear why not. While mental-health officials would present the testimony of mental-health professionals about the need for continued intensive care and commitment, the committed patient's lawyer may cross-examine those professionals, offer contrary test results and records, and also call witnesses, including even other mental-health professionals, to prove that the patient has no further need of commitment. Ordinarily, though, care providers and patient representatives will agree, and after a period of a few days or perhaps weeks, the commitment will end with a court order approving the patient's release.

Be sure that your niece and her parents or guardians understand her right to hearing and representation. They should be consulting a lawyer with expertise in this area if they have any doubt around her commitment, care, and release. Your niece has an important social asset in your interest and the care and interest of other family members. Keep being an advocate for her care.

36

When Influence Is a Bad Thing

Question

My sister-in-law is suddenly taking a very keen interest in mom's financial and legal affairs, as mom's health declines. Mom even said something about their having been to the lawyer's office the other day, when mom otherwise never gets out. Mom had her will and everything else in good order after dad died. What's up?

Answer

Maybe nothing, but consider checking it out now with mom, sister-in-law, and other family members. Better to be on the same page now than to face a probate dispute later.

Your concern is a legitimate one that as mom declines she needs more care but also becomes subject to greater influence. It is natural that your mother might require assistance with her financial affairs. Making deposits, paying bills, and keeping a checkbook can become onerous tasks as mental and physical abilities decline. Your sister-in-law may simply be doing your mother a good turn. Even a visit to the probate lawyer late in life may be perfectly innocent. Your mother may have wished to

201

provide specially for a new grandchild or a certain charity, or satisfy another legitimate interest having no advantage to your sister-in-law.

Yet in the worst case, mom might sign legal and financial documents that she does not understand or consent to things with which she does not agree, because of pressure or other coercive influences from your sister-in-law or others. You are concerned that mom would get out and visit a lawyer when her legal affairs were already in order. As long as your mother remains competent, she may manage her legal affairs as she wishes, without necessarily disclosing them to you or other family members. But if she did previously disclose them to you and other family members after your father's passing, then it might well be unusual that she would make changes to her estate plan now without equal disclosure. Without accusing anyone of anything, respectfully share your concern with interested family members, particularly your sister-in-law. You may be able to address your concern without the law's help.

The law will help when others exercise undue influence over a weakened and vulnerable testator to alter a will and estate plan. State probate laws authorize a probate court to set aside a will, codicil (amendment) to a will, or other estate-plan documents when the testator executed them under another's undue influence. Probate courts will hold hearings, taking testimony and other evidence to determine whether to accept the contested will or other estate document. Will contests arise particularly when the testator made a late change to an estate plan at a beneficiary's behest without the knowledge or support of others who lost their own beneficiary interest because of the late change. An undue-influence claim requires that the challenger prove the influence, the execution of documents under that influence, and that but for the influence the testator would have made or kept other plans.

Courts often look to the nature of the relationship between the testator and influencer, and how natural was the new disposition that the influenced testator made. A testator who secretly leaves everything to a housekeeper at the last moment may well have suffered the housekeeper's influence, whereas a testator who openly divides everything equally among adult children well before death probably suffered none. Courts will often consider the natural objects of the testator's uninfluenced affections. Children and grandchildren are natural objects of affection, as might be a long-loved charity. Paid housekeepers and care providers, and non-family interlopers, are less often so. Isolation from family, secretiveness, weakness of mind, and disposition of assets to the person exercising the influence are all undue-influence factors.

So again, meet with your sister-in-law, mom, and other family members to discuss the subject of your mom's estate plan. If you cannot get the answers that you feel you need, and your mom passes away leaving an altered estate plan that you do not respect, then consult a lawyer about an undue-influence claim.

35

Oh, Please Release Me

Question

My daughter had a minor fender-bender the other day that barely damaged the other car. Its driver-owner agreed to take $500 from me so that I could avoid an insurance claim. I want the driver-owner to promise not to make the insurance claim or to sue. What do I do?

Answer

Have the driver-owner sign a properly drafted release of all claims.

Your effort to resolve the matter probably makes sense, especially if your daughter was to blame for the collision. State law determines the obligation of one driver to another or to the vehicle owner with respect to vehicle damage or other injury. Most states recognize negligence claims, although a few no-fault states limit those claims to small amounts, granting limited immunity to at-fault drivers. Depending on your state's law, if your daughter was careless in failing to observe, yield, or stop, and caused the collision, then she probably owes the driver-owner for the damage. Again depending on your state's law, particularly whether you are in a no-fault state, your daughter could also owe damages for personal injuries to the driver-owner. Other owners or registrants of your daughter's vehicle, if she did not own her vehicle alone, may also owe the same liability under owner-consent laws.

Your daughter's motor-vehicle insurance should cover the liability, depending on your state's law and the policy that she purchased. Your daughter could simply turn the matter over to her insurer for investigation and defense of the claim, and its payment. On the other hand, an insurance claim on a policy issued to a young driver can increase the young driver's premium substantially. If the vehicle's driver-owner is willing to accept your $500 not to make a claim, then you and the driver-owner must feel that the agreement is fair under all the circumstances. The vehicle's damage may be more than $500. The driver-owner may have suffered some undetected injury. If the driver-owner is willing to accept your $500 while taking those risks that the repairs will cost more or that the driver-owner has some other loss or injury, then good for you.

State laws routinely recognize releases of rights except in a few special circumstances not applicable here. A release is essentially a contract, meaning an agreement between the party who pays and the party who gives up the right in exchange for payment. Releases should be in writing, dated, and signed by at least the party who is giving up the rights. The party making the payment also sometimes will sign the release. The key with any release, though, is to describe adequately the rights that the party intends to give up. Does the release include only property damage or also personal injury? Does the release include only known claims and injuries or also unknown claims and injuries that the injured party may discover in the future? A poor description may leave unreleased rights still in the hands of the party suffering the injury or damage, and may leave the proverbial door open for that party later to sue.

Thus here, your writing should describe not only vehicle damage but probably damage to contents of the vehicle and injury to its occupants, particularly the owner-driver. You both may think that only the vehicle suffered damage and the only damage that it suffered was a bent fender. Later, the owner-driver may discover damage to the vehicle's systems or contents, or injuries to himself. Don't be surprised. Accident injuries, particularly neck and back injuries, can take a few days or even much longer to manifest themselves fully. That delay in discovery is one reason that some insurers will pay small amounts to settle claims quickly. As the paying party, you would want the release to include known and unknown claims, known and unknown damage, and known and unknown injuries.

With a signed release describing the released claims broadly, you should be all set. Get the signature on the release at the same time that you convey the settlement funds so that you have no disagreement later over the terms of the settlement. A few states permit parties who sign releases to return the money and set aside the release within a defined period such as 30 days, especially if they discover more-serious loss or injury. From the sounds of it, you shouldn't be too worried about that. Consult a lawyer if you have any doubt. And report the matter to your daughter's insurer promptly the moment that you have any reason to believe that the claim is more serious than a minor fender-bender. Your daughter's insurance policy very likely requires prompt notice and cooperation, or the insurer may be able to void the policy.

And no more fender-benders.

34

Slip or Trip and Fall

Question

The weather has been a little wintry recently, leaving some ice and snow on the driveway and walks around my home. If I have a dinner party at my home at which someone falls, am I going to be sued for everything I own?

Answer

Probably not, but let's think about it.

First, if you own rather than rent your home, then you probably insure it, especially if you have a mortgage, in which case your lender would require insurance. You probably think of homeowner's insurance as applying to fire or other damage to the home. Yet homeowner's insurance typically includes liability coverage up to a certain limit, say, $250,000, $300,000, or $500,000. If a social guest suffered injury at your home and sued you over that injury, then your homeowner's insurance would likely hire a lawyer to defend you and then pay any settlement or judgment up to the insurance limits. You would only pay if the settlement or judgment exceeded those limits. Not many fall injuries result in damages exceeding typical limits.

Insurance is only your first line of defense. Consider next whether you would owe anything at all. State law governs premises liability. States differ in those laws. Traditionally, the law would first classify the person who suffers injury on your property. If that person was a trespasser, for example, then the landowner would owe little or no duty to prevent the trespasser's harm while trespassing on the property. Naturally, we owe trespassers the least of duties because they have legal right even to be on the land. If instead as you have indicated the injured person was a social guest, known to the law as a *licensee*, then traditionally you would have liability to the social guest only if you knew of a hidden danger that you failed to disclose to the guest. Snow or ice, though, is not usually a hidden danger.

If instead the injured person is a customer or other *business invitee* as the law calls it, then traditionally you would have liability to the invitee if you did not exercise reasonable care as to the invitee's safety, such as by clearing snowy drives and walks and salting icy drives and walks. We owe the highest duty to business invitees because we attract, expect, desire, and benefit from their presence on the land. Other states simply hold that landowners owe the same duty of reasonable care to all persons on the land, even trespassers, although one might still consider the reason for and expectation of their entry.

Even if you did breach a duty to your social guest or invitee, then the law may still provide you with defenses to that liability. Some states reject landowner liability when the danger is open and obvious to the claimant, meaning readily observable from casual inspection. Snow and ice is usually readily observable. Some states also have natural-accumulation rules as to snow and ice, meaning that if the snow and ice was nothing more than that which fell out of the sky, made no worse by human intervention, then the landowner has no liability. The states also recognize comparative or contributory fault on the part of the social guest or invitee, reducing or barring the recovery.

The same rules would apply to trip-and-fall cases as to slip-and-fall and other premises-liability cases. In general, one looks for an unreasonably dangerous defect in the condition of the premises, such as badly cracked sidewalks, loose treads on steps, unraveling rugs on which one might catch a heel, and so on. A visitor has no automatic right of recovery from the landowner but must instead prove the condition that caused the fall while also proving that the premises were not reasonably safe. So when you expect visitors of any kind, take a look around. Think of their safety. Not only is doing so a good way to avoid liability, it is also a good way to avoid injury. You don't want your guests hurt.

33

Reading the Fine Print

Question

Every once in a while I get one of these hard-to-read legal notices in the mail saying that I may get some money from somewhere someday for something that I once bought. I've never gotten anything yet but, like the thousands of others who apparently get the same notices, I'm still hoping. What are these notices?

Answer

You are probably describing a class-action notice. If you are a qualifying member of the class and the action results in a settlement or judgment, then you may be entitled to recover class-action damages. Next time, read the notice carefully and comply with any elections or information that it requires for you to become a class member and receive a portion of any settlement or judgment. If you don't understand the notice, then consult with a lawyer.

Class actions are how the courts handle litigation where the claimants (the parties suffering injury or loss) are too numerous to manage efficiently. Federal law expands federal-court jurisdiction for class actions, and federal rules accommodate those actions. The class members' claims must raise common issues of law and fact, and the few class members actually named in the suit must represent the class adequately. Class actions must also show in one of several different ways that they are superior means over individual resolution. The courts rather jealously guard their class-action jurisdiction, certifying as class actions only those cases that meet class-action rules' strict requirements.

Those notices that you receive follow the court's certification of the class action. The parties and court must at that point determine who is in or out of the class because the action may determine finally important rights of potential class members. Some notices, called *opt in*, require you to respond indicating that you wish to join the class. Other notices, called *opt out*, require no response, instead assuming that you are a class member unless you respond indicating that you are not. Opt in or opt out often effectively determines the size of the class because relatively few notice recipients respond to notices. You may opt in or opt out, but chances are good that you won't do either, making the form of the notice the critical determinant.

The parties will then litigate the class action much like ordinary actions through a period of discovery and pretrial procedure up to and through trial of one or more representative claims. In general, if the representative wins, then you, the class member, win. If the representative loses, then you, the class member, lose. While the class action may not be perfectly fair because of small differences in individual claims, the court and parties save trying dozens, hundreds, or even thousands of cases. Asbestos and tobacco litigation are examples. Tens of thousands of individuals would have had such claims, but the courts have entertained and tried or settled only a relative handful of class-action cases.

Class actions also settle after hearing and approval by the court. Some class-action settlements have been controversial for winning the lawyers substantial fees while winning the class members modest coupons, credits, or other nominal recovery or rights. On the other hand, class actions can cost the lawyers substantial time and money, and carry substantial risk. They are also often the only way of holding national corporations accountable for small wrongs that to any one class member make little difference but collectively undermine consumer confidence and rights. The court will provide class members bound by the settlement a second notice.

So, once again, read the notice, or get a lawyer's help to do so. Class actions are not quite like the lottery. They serve both public- and private-justice purposes. But if you read and follow the notices, a class action can feel like winning the lottery, bringing something for nothing.

32

Long Waits at the Border

Question

I don't like flying in and out of the country anymore. Getting through the lines with your passport and luggage is just one big headache. And then all the questions that they ask, making you feel like a criminal suspect. I mean, I understand terrorism and all that, but why all the fuss?

Answer

You got it. Like it or not, national security has a lot to do with border security. Better get used to the lines and questions, unless you want to swim the Rio Grande or sneak across miles of desert at night to re-enter the country illegally. Even U.S. citizens must produce lawful documentation for re-entry.

While luggage inspection for weapons or bombs, and terrorist surveillance and investigation, are critically important functions, law provides the backbone of national security. You may leave the country at any time, provided that another country will let you enter. Unless you are certain of the other country's entry requirements, before leaving the U.S., you should check with the

213

other country's consulate or embassy to see what entry documentation it may require. Even if you are a U.S. citizen, you still implicate U.S. national security when you attempt to re-enter the United States. Immigration laws require documentation of your right to enter and remain in the United States legally. Just because you left as a U.S. citizen does not mean that you may re-enter the United States without documentation. You have the same obligation to show documentation as any other entrant, whether or not a citizen.

U.S. officials have been issuing between about 10 million and 20 million passports each year for the past several years, fluctuating widely but generally representing at least a doubling of the passport issuances of prior years. Many more of us are traveling with passports. Your passport represents your legal standing to re-enter the country. It will not only show that you are a U.S. citizen but also likely identify other countries that you visited when leaving. Border officials may use those identifying marks to determine what investigation if any to make of you on your re-entry.

Border officials offer a Mobile Passport Control app for your smartphone to automate and speed the process of inspecting your passport for re-entry. U.S. military identification with travel orders and U.S. Merchant Mariner documentation when on official business will also facilitate re-entry into the United States. At some entry locations, border officials will also recognize not just passports but passport cards, trusted-traveler cards like NEXUS, SENTRI, and FAST, or even an enhanced driver's license. Check on these requirements *before* you leave if you intend to enter with anything other than a current U.S. passport. Lawful permanent residents who do not have a U.S. passport will present their U.S. permanent-resident card. Foreign travelers entering the U.S. with a passport or other documentation from another country will follow US-VISIT biometric procedures ensuring through digital finger or face scans that they are who their documentation claims they are.

U.S. Customs and Border Protection officials are responsible for your border and customs inspection. Customs inspection does not have to do with national security but international trade. The U.S. and other countries assess duties or tariffs on certain goods entering the country. When you bring into the U.S. items that you purchased abroad, you must declare those items at the border. Depending on the nature, value, and source of those items, you may pay to bring them into the country. For example, for goods you purchase in Mexico or Canada to bring into the U.S., you have an exemption up to $800 from duties on gifts and personal items. The Customs and Border Protection agency does offer a Global Entry program to speed your way through customs. You must register for the program before attempting re-entry and then use the special Global Entry kiosks to obtain a transaction receipt that should speed your re-entry. The Global Entry program relieves you from the obligation to complete the paper customs-declaration form required of other travelers.

Sure, re-entry can be a lot of fuss, but national security and customs laws warrant inspection and circumspection. Be patient. America is a reasonably secure and very prosperous country. The border wait is worth it.

31

Whose Law Is It, Anyway?

Question

I keep hearing that some U.S. courts are starting to follow international or foreign law instead of our law. That just does not make sense to me. Can international or foreign law really trump American law?

Answer

Not truly in the manner about which you may be concerned. Yet U.S. courts do apply international law in cases that international norms govern and the law of foreign jurisdictions when choice-of-law rules require them to do so. Also, foreign law has long influenced the common law applied in U.S. courts. The question is more complex than you may realize. You probably have little to fear about foreign or international law displacing U.S. law on domestic issues.

The U.S. Constitution ensures that it and the federal laws enacted under it remain the supreme law of the land. The Constitution's Article VI says so, that the Constitution, federal laws made under the Constitution, and treaties that the United

States makes, are the supreme law of the land to which "the judges in every state shall be bound thereby, anything in the Constitution or laws of any State to the contrary notwithstanding." You may have noticed that this Supremacy Clause, as we call it, includes treaties as the supreme law of the land. The Supreme Court recently clarified that while the United States may make international commitments under certain treaties, those international commitments do not become binding domestic law unless self-executing as such or Congress enacts implementing statutes. The Supreme Court has resisted converting international commitments into domestic strictures.

That said, federal courts in the U.S. and also some U.S. state courts frequently hear and decide cases involving foreign transactions, incidents, and parties. When you think about it, those foreign cases should not surprise you because of the global travels of U.S. citizens and the global reach of U.S. corporations and interests. If you suffered an injury or loss in Italy while on vacation, then you still might want to seek redress in U.S. courts rather than Italian courts for that injury or loss, particularly if the person or entity responsible for it had U.S. bank accounts, property, insurance, or other connections. U.S. courts also entertain contract, licensing, or other transactional disputes arising out of foreign matters, as long as those matters have some connection with U.S. parties or interests. Foreign parties and matters are no strangers in U.S. courts, particularly in parts of the country like New York and Los Angeles where international trade and travel are prevalent.

In those foreign cases, foreign law may well apply, even though the U.S. court would administer the case and apply the foreign law. Courts follow choice-of-law rules to know which law applies. For instance, sometimes a New York court will apply the law of Florida or vice versa if the case has more contacts with the other state and the other state has more-substantial interests. The same is true for foreign jurisdictions. If a New York court entertains a case involving an accident in Spain, then the New

York court may well apply Spanish law because of the accident's location in Spain and Spain's more-substantial safety or other public interest in the case's outcome. In short, U.S. courts apply the law that makes the most sense for the case after considering factors like the connections and interests.

You would not under those choice-of-law rules see a U.S. court decide a domestic divorce, child-custody case, or motor-vehicle accident using foreign law. Instead, the court would very likely apply the law of the U.S. state in which the event took place, that is, its own law. The vast majority of cases in most U.S. state courts involve purely domestic matters in which the courts give no thought to anything other than U.S. law. Choice-of-law rules are generally not controversial. They are instead meant to be non-controversial, to do the sensible and even obvious thing.

That is not to say that foreign law never has any influence on U.S. courts. It does. American courts applying the common law have to some degree always considered foreign law, particularly the common law of England, which may not seem like a foreign country but nonetheless is. Nearer the country's founding, the Supreme Court and state appellate courts would often look to English common law for the controlling legal principles. Even today, though, the Supreme Court has referred to foreign laws and precedent to inform, if not to outright govern, its decisions on U.S. constitutional law, which may be the practice to which you are referring. Yet in those relatively rare instances, those foreign laws do not tell us what U.S. law must be but instead simply suggest what U.S. law could or should be.

Any less concerned? Maybe not. We do live in a global age, but the Constitution still guards our laws. With vigilance toward the Constitution, we should be alright.

30

You're How Old?

Question

I have a bartender friend who just got in trouble for serving a drink to an underage minor and a co-worker under investigation for having sex with an underage minor. I just don't understand it. Who's to know how old someone really is?

Answer

That's exactly it. You are supposed to find out — reliably, with proof of age, not just on their word — before permitting a minor to engage in certain risky conduct.

State legislatures place age limits on conduct that, while acceptable for a consenting adult who understands better the risks and consequences, appears too risky, corrupting, and potentially harmful for minors. The young in varying degrees lack experience, self-control, self-insight, and judgment. Driving a motor vehicle, operating a motorboat, and hunting with a gun are reasonably safe and healthy activities from which we nonetheless restrict the young. The concerns over the ability of youth to handle an activity compound when the activity has a demonstrably or potentially harmful or corrupting dimension to it.

Smoking, drinking alcohol, and sexual intimacy fall readily into this class of concerns. State laws place age limits on each of those activities. State legislatures intend these laws to protect the minor whom the legislatures judge too young to consent wisely to the conduct. Drinking, particularly in binges or to other excess, can be harmful to your health and dangerous to yourself and others. Underage drinking is a major public health problem with thousands of youths dying every year from it. Smoking is harmful to your health and to others near you. Underage smoking is also a major health problem, addicting minors who continue to smoke throughout their lifetimes. Sex can corrupt relationships, psyches, and behavior, lead to mental and physical abuse, and transmit incurably fatal or loathsome disease. Legislatures properly take these concerns seriously, so seriously that they not only regulate the behavior of youths but also provide for punishing the adult who facilitates the youthful transgression.

State laws against underage drinking regulate both the commercial establishment and social setting. Bars can lose their liquor licenses and bartenders suffer criminal charges for serving the underage minor. Liquor laws require bars and bartenders to confirm lawful drinking age with reliable identification, known colloquially as *carding*. State laws may also make illegal serving minors in social settings. The same is true for dispensing cigarettes to minors, that laws prohibit sales to minors while also prohibiting adults from buying cigarettes for or supplying cigarettes to minors.

State legislatures reserve the most-serious charges, though, for adults who solicit and have sex with underage minors. The intimacy may have been consensual in the usual way that participants think of consent, meaning without physical force overcoming the will of one of the participants. Yet lawyers and judges refer to the crime as *statutory rape*, not to exaggerate the violence but because the concept of consent loses its meaning around sex with minors. The superiority and influence of the adult, the subordinate role and weakness of the minor, and the power of sexual attraction combine to make consent impossible or meaningless. Conviction for the crime can carry sentence much like forcible rape of an adult. Statutory rape is very serious crime.

You are right that these laws tend to place the risk that the youth is in fact underage squarely on the adult, not relieving the adult from guilt if the youth falsely stated an older age or looked sufficiently mature not to be underage or even close to it. One suspects that if the law were otherwise, that a simple statement by the youth that the youth was older created a defense to the charge, then we would have far fewer convictions. Some of the reason for the laws putting the risk of mistaken age on the adult may be that the parties would otherwise too easily manipulate the circumstances to defeat conviction. Youths might routinely claim older age in these solicitous encounters or at least testify later to having done so under pressure from the suspect adult.

But the simpler policy reason for shifting the underage risk to the participating adult may be that adults should after all be in charge of the situation and know better. The sense may simply be shame on any adult who lets an underage minor convince them to share alcohol, cigarettes, or sex. Blaming the corruption on the kid is hardly responsible. So, yes, you are to know how old the kid is, no matter what the kid may say. Be adult. Be responsible.

29

Zoned Out

Question

I am so tired of fighting City Hall over what I want to do with my own property. I can't replace a window or door, or put up a sign, without their review and approval, no less build something new at my location. I feel like *they* are designing my place rather than *me* designing it, and I even have to pay them for the reviews. What gives the city so much zoning power?

Answer

As a former president famously said, I feel your pain. Zoning restrictions and building codes have grown more sophisticated, complex, and precise, requiring property owners to work ever more closely with zoning and building officials. If you have the sense that you are in a partnership now with those officials, rather than master of your own castle, then you have the right sense. You have only modest protection from the law against extensive land-use and other building restrictions.

The technical answer to your question is that state legislation authorizes local zoning measures, while local-government representatives then decide what those measures will be, adopting the local zoning provisions. Some local communities, particularly but not exclusively those in rural areas, have little or no zoning restrictions. Other communities, particularly though not exclusive in urban or other heavily populated areas, have extensive zoning restrictions, especially around business and historic districts. The window, door, and sign restrictions to which you refer probably have to do with business-district classification. Historic districts may be even more restrictive in preventing

Zoning measures often have public health and safety as their motivating purposes, for instance recognizing floodplains and drainage districts. Creating zones for industrial and commercial uses, and segregating those zones from residential and recreational uses, can ensure that traffic, crowds, noise, smoke, dust, odors, and other conditions associated with that commerce do not interfere with residential and recreational uses. Economics, development, and infrastructure also play roles in justifying zoning districts. Farmland districts preserve open lands against piecemeal and encroaching development. Industrial districts efficiently concentrate water, sewer, and road infrastructure, while commercial districts attract the diverse retail mix necessary to sustain customer traffic. Yet establishing or preserving character and aesthetics can also justify districts, especially when the purpose is to preserve historic or unique character.

Despite the broad authority local government finds in state law to regulate land use through zoning provisions, law can nonetheless provide some protection against overzealous local officials imposing onerous restrictions. The U.S. Constitution's 14th Amendment guarantees property owners equal protection and due process of law with respect to zoning provisions. Local officials must not act arbitrarily or capriciously when imposing those restrictions. If, for instance, officials permit others to ignore zoning restrictions, then those officials may not be able to enforce them against the next property owner in a discriminatory fashion. Zoning officials must also give fair notice of the restrictions and an opportunity for hearing for relief from or correction of a zoning decision. When zoning imposes such a burden as to deprive an owner of all economic use of property, the owner may pursue a takings claim against local government for just compensation. Property owners pursue these rights in court actions.

Consult a lawyer with expertise in land-use regulation, when you face what you believe to be unduly onerous restrictions, especially those for which local officials cannot give satisfactory explanation. Working closely with legal counsel and an architect, planner, or other professional skilled in regulatory design issues may not only get you the official permission you need but also get you a better design. Zoning restrictions often seem onerous but should always have a beneficial purpose. Recognizing and pursuing that beneficial purpose may be to your own advantage. If good-faith efforts at compliance fail, then ask your lawyer whether the zoning restrictions are lawful. If not, then you should be able to win relief. City Hall should not be picking fights.

28

The Bombs Bursting in Air

Question

Every year we have to travel to the neighboring state to buy our fireworks for the 4th of July. Then, we always end up buying the fireworks from roadside vendors in tents. What's the big deal with selling or not selling fireworks?

Answer

Gee, don't know if you noticed or not, but fireworks can be a little dangerous. States and municipalities either regulate them heavily, including by and to whom the fireworks sell, or ban them outright. That's why you have to drive to the next state and buy from a tent vendor.

Federal laws enacted under the Commerce Clause regulate the sale of hazardous substances including fireworks. To carry those federal laws into effect, the federal Consumer Products Safety Commission has promulgated regulations requiring fireworks makers to meet construction, performance, and warning standards. Federal investigators collect and test fireworks, not only from domestic retailers and manufacturers but also importers, and ban them as hazardous substances if they do not meet those standards. Fireworks, you can see, are serious business.

Beyond those federal enactments, under the U.S. Constitution, the states retain legal authority to enact general laws regulating health, safety, and welfare. A handful of Northeast states including populous New York ban fireworks outright. A handful of additional Midwest and Northeast states limit firework sales to stick sparklers and similar small novelties. The rest of the states permit most fireworks sales, as long as the fireworks meet the federal regulations. Those states, though, may ban sales to minors while also prohibiting firework use by the intoxicated or on public or private property without permission. Some also require a state or local license to sell fireworks, further requiring that sellers obtain insurance relating to their sale. Interestingly, states also often regulate the time and dates of sale, typically only in the days leading right up to Independence Day. Once again, fireworks are serious business.

Your city or county may also have something to say about whether and when you can sell, buy, or display fireworks. Some states preempt local regulation of fireworks while other states authorize or permit local regulation. Some local regulations permit only public displays of fireworks, and many more restrict their use only to certain periods. Quite a few also ban them entirely. Violating state or local laws could result in fines or even jail. If you do not have the skill or inclination to research these requirements, then consider contacting your local fire department. That's right. Your local fire department will likely be quite familiar with the regulation, use, and consequences of fireworks. Of course, violating laws and acting carelessly with fireworks while causing injury can result in civil liability for those injuries. Once again, fireworks are risky business.

Oh, and one last warning. You know that practice of yours of carrying fireworks across state lines? Be careful. You may well be breaking your own state's law when you bring them across the state line. Police officials know the practice of vendors to sell right across the state line. They regularly take enforcement action at the state border during the peak times for sale, confiscating tons of fireworks and charging the unwitting possessor with state crimes. Fireworks, though fun to many, are serious and risky business.

27

Is Email Ever Private?

Question

My boss seems to know more of what's going on with my co-workers and me than my boss should know. Rumor has it that the IT Department reads and shares our email whenever the boss wants. Do employees have any privacy in their email anymore?

Answer

You may have some privacy, but it probably depends on your employer's computer-use policy. Federal and state laws can protect your personal communications, particularly if your employer consents to personal use of workplace email systems. On the other hand, if the employer reliably publishes a clear policy that it monitors your workplace electronic communications, then you likely have only very limited privacy rights. As many as half of employers monitor employee email under such policies, and as many as a quarter of employers have terminated employees over email misuse.

The primary federal law affecting these rights is the Stored Wire and Electronic Communications and Transactional Records Act, often referred to as the Stored Communications Act. Congress presumably directed the Act toward hackers and spies, but its coverage is sufficiently broad to implicate employers and others who access messages on remote servers. Under the Act, employers and others must not intentionally access certain electronic communications without authorization or exceeding granted authorization. Depending on some specifics, these restrictions can mean that employers must not read employee email or, if an employer has the authorization to monitor its own email system, must nonetheless stop reading an employee's email as soon as recognizing that it is private rather than work related. The Act carries criminal penalties, giving employers and others good reason for pause when monitoring employee email.

Similarly, state privacy laws can limit employers from intruding on an employee's seclusion, where the intrusion would be highly offensive to the reasonable person, and from public disclosure of private facts. Electronic communications with family, friends, medical care providers, financial advisors, and others can be highly personal. Employer access to those communications could be highly embarrassing and offensive. Employers can limit these privacy rights, though, by keeping employees informed about the monitoring and inspection of electronic equipment and records. The *expectation* of privacy is an important factor in whether a person will actually *have* privacy in any particular setting. If an employer informs employees that email and other electronic records are subject to frequent review and searches, then employees have less of a privacy interest. Public and private employers notify employees that computers remain the property of the employer and that the employer may inspect all files and emails using the employer's equipment and systems.

Privacy laws can be complex and their application highly case specific. Federal and state wiretapping and eavesdropping laws may apply to certain types of telephone or electronic monitoring. Federal and state statutes also grant specific privacy rights in medical records, Social Security numbers, and other information, adding to the complexity of privacy rights. States are also enacting statutes that prevent employers from requiring employees to share passwords for their social media accounts. So you do have some rights, although again, your employer's policies will go a long way toward determining just how extensive are those rights. If you have a genuine and deep concern that your employer is invading your privacy by accessing your private and confidential emails, email attachments, or other electronic records, then consult a lawyer who has expertise in this area.

26

Marching to the Beat of Another Drummer

Question

I've been hearing about military courts and court martial, not just for disobeying an officer or going AWOL but for all kinds of other small and large things. It sounds like servicemembers have their own courts and laws. How does that work?

Answer

Servicemembers indeed serve under a military justice system that parallels and in some cases duplicates or overlaps state laws that apply to the general population. Military members follow their own code while also subject to the laws applying to the general population.

The U.S. Constitution grants Congress the sole authority to raise and support an army and navy, meaning to form and govern the military services. Congress has carried out that responsibility in part by putting in place the Uniform Code of Military Justice and other statutes dictating limits on servicemembers' conduct. The Code of Military Justice applies to all servicemembers whether the country is at peace or war and the servicemember serves domestically or abroad. Regulations authorized by the President as Commander in Chief of the Armed Forces and a common law of military customs round out the Code of Military Justice into a detailed and comprehensive set of laws governing servicemembers on active duty, in the reserve and Guard, or retired.

Commanding officers are typically the first line of Code enforcement. Commanding officers may authorize searches, and arrest and detention of a suspected violator, and then refer the violator to court martial where the commanding officer may pursue or dismiss charges. Court martials are similar to civilian courts but staffed entirely by military members. Commanding officers have the authority not only to convene a court martial but to select its members acting as the jury. While commanding officers have substantial authority, they must follow the Code's procedures and procedures set forth in the Manual for Courts Martial and Manual of the Judge Advocate General. Of course, commanding officers may also impose non-Code punishments to bring the servicemember into line.

Many Military Code of Justice provisions are peculiar to military service, like fraudulent enlistment, desertion, absence without leave, contempt toward officials, disrespect of an officer, failure to obey an order, aiding the enemy, spying, misbehaving while a sentinel, and unauthorized detention or release of a prisoner. These are not crimes that general codes would include. Other Military Code of Justice provisions are like laws applying to the general population, such as murder, manslaughter, drunk or reckless driving, rape, robbery, larceny, assault, burglary, resisting arrest, forgery, and writing a bad check. One could see these charges in a military court martial or in a civilian court. The

232

Supreme Court has held that a servicemember's service connection is enough to charge and try the servicemember in a court martial for a non-service-related crime, for instance one occurring off base.

Violating the Military Code of Justice can result in simple loss of certain military privileges, or confinement in a military detention facility, or discharge from military service. Punishments can be severe. The Military Code of Justice provides for the death penalty and also for life in prison without parole. Recent death-penalty convictions have been for premeditated murder or murder while committing another felony, much like one would see in civilian courts. When a servicemember suffers criminal conviction in a civilian court, a commanding officer may impose military discipline for the civilian transgression. The two systems of justice, military and civilian, can and do overlap, with civilian and military courts having dual jurisdiction over many crimes that servicemembers commit. Nothing like having two masters.

25

One Free Bite

Question

The neighborhood's canine scourge just bit another child. I am so tired of these snarling animals threatening everyone in the neighborhood. People who own dogs, especially biting dogs, should be more responsible. What does the law have to say about it?

Answer

Plenty. Owners of biting dogs generally pay for the harm done and may also lose the dog.

Dog-bite law is state law, varying some from state to state. The traditional common law having to do with dog bites generally holds a dog-owner liable for the harm due to the bite only if the owner knew that the dog had vicious propensities abnormal to its class. Some cases refer to this rule as the *one-bite rule* because until the dog bites (or growls or snarls) once, the owner may have no knowledge of any vicious propensities. Get it — one free bite? On the second bite (a bite of another person after the owner knows that the dog bit the first person), the owner will be strictly liable and have to pay damages to the bitten person. Homeowner's insurance has a liability coverage that would typically cover dog-bite damages, so that the dog-owner homeowner might actually pay little or nothing out of pocket.

Statutes in many states, though, modify the one-bite rule and instead make the dog's owner or keeper strictly liable for the first and any subsequent bite. Under those statutes, the owner's knowledge of the dog's propensity to bite makes no difference. The policy is simply to shift the bite risk to the dog's owner who, after all, has the greater opportunity to leash, chain, pen, or otherwise secure the dog to eliminate the possibility that it will bite. The statutes typically offer a defense to the dog's owner only if the person bitten was trespassing at the time of the bite or provoked the dog into biting, in which cases (one supposes the legislatures were concluding) dogs ought to bite.

States and municipalities have other dog laws. Many locales have leash laws, requiring owners to keep dogs on a leash whenever outdoors where they would otherwise be free to roam. Violation of the leash law could result not only in a civil infraction and fine but also negligence liability for any injury the unleashed dog might cause, such as by running into and knocking over people or bicycles, or chasing cars. Trust me. Those injuries happen. Other laws can require that local officials (think *dogcatcher*) impound the biting dog for several days until they can determine that the dog did not have rabies at the time of the bite. Those officials may then seek a court or administrative order for the dog's destruction if investigation proves its severe propensity to bite. The dog's owner would have the due-process right to challenge the evidence of that propensity.

You are right to be concerned and that dog owners should be responsible. Dog-bite injuries can be serious, even lethal. Several victims die each year in the United States from bites from several different breeds of large, medium, and even small dogs. A dog bite can scar the victim physically, mentally, and emotionally. It is hard not to blame the dog especially when it is consistently

235

vicious, but truly, dog owners bear the greater part of the responsibility. The law certainly treats it that way. Tell your neighbors to control their dogs. If they don't, and the dogs present a threat to the neighborhood's safety, then contact local law-enforcement officials. Laws are all about health, safety, and welfare. As much as we love them, dogs are no exception.

24

Think Before You Jump

Question

My buddies and I went whitewater rafting recently. You should have seen the paper they had us sign before we got in the water. It had more fine print than the telephone book. Anyway, nothing bad happened to any of us, but if it had, would we have been able to sue?

Answer

Probably not. Next time, read the fine print. Or pick a safer recreation.

Some of the recreational activities in which we engage are just so hazardous that you cannot avoid substantial risk. In fact, those hazards are why we pursue those activities. Bungee jumping from a bridge into a deep canyon over rushing waters, base jumping from a cliff to the rock plain hundreds of feet below, and whitewater rafting all come to mind as dangerous but accepted recreations, at least in places. Yet recreations as seemingly tame as canoeing, kayaking, and scuba diving also carry significant risks of injury even with reasonable care in their preparation and performance. People are going to get injured.

The companies and individuals who sponsor and conduct those activities must thoughtfully allocate the risk of injury as to those activities. Insurance is one way of allocating risk, by shifting it from the insured to the insurer. Yet some of these recreational activities are so dangerous that insurance would be prohibitively expensive without more thought to allocating the natural and unavoidable risk of injury. If you were an insurer, then would you underwrite bungee or base jumping? Probably not. So the thought is that if people want to do dangerous things, then let them, and others will even help them do so, but then the people engaging in the dangerous activities should carry the risk of their own injury, especially when the proprietors are unable to afford or find insurance.

That point is where a release of liability comes in. State laws govern injury claims, just as they govern releases of injury claims. Many states permit a participant to release certain claims against the sponsor or conductor of an activity in advance of those claims arising. The fine-print document you signed was very probably just such a release. If you had read it, then you would likely have seen that you were promising not to sue the whitewater-rafting company for your injury whether or not the company was in some respect careless. Claimants typically rely on negligence (carelessness) theories when making liability claims. Ordinarily, if you could show that the proprietor should in the exercise of reasonable care have done something more to protect you but did not do so, and you were injured as a result, then the proprietor would have liability to pay you for your damages. But when you signed the release, you likely gave up those claims.

Under some state laws, fine print may not be enough to protect the proprietor of these activities. State laws may require that proprietors requiring releases of claims ensure that they reasonably notify you of the risks of the activity you are facing. Written releases should be clear. You may also have noticed signs or heard the guides giving other warnings. State laws may also prohibit a proprietor from obtaining a release of recklessness or intentional-misconduct claims. It is one thing to relieve a company of liability for carelessness but quite another thing to let someone get off for committing an intentional harm. State laws generally do not permit releases of intentional or willful or wanton harm. States disagree on whether a parent may waive future claims on behalf of their children.

You might have thought of refusing to sign the release, in which case the proprietor would probably have refused to let you onto the raft. You might also have thought of reading and striking portions of the release. If you had attempted to do so, though, then you would probably have had to bring your modifications to the attention of someone in charge who had the authority to accept them. Contract law, which releases are, abhors sneakiness. Fine print is bad enough. The parties should be agreeing on the terms. If you don't like the risks or the shifting of the risks, then don't participate. If you participate, then you are probably participating on the terms to which you agree when you sign. If it ever truly matters to you, as for instance if you are ever injured in such a circumstance, then have a lawyer check it out. And think before you raft or leap.

23

Recording with the Register

Question

I'm thinking of buying a place on a land contract. A friend of mine who is a real-estate agent gave me a land-contract form that should work but also said something about recording a memorandum of land contract. When I asked him what he meant, he said something about the Register of Deeds. What's that?

Answer

The Register of Deeds is where you go to find out who holds what interest in what lands.

A register-of-deeds office is a state statutory office usually formed at the county level. State law provides for registers of deeds. The county would locate the register-of-deeds office at the county seat, possibly in the courthouse or another county administrative building. The Register of Deeds is not a court function, although frequently enough one finds disputes in court over land ownership involving documents that the Register of Deeds recorded. Recording is how the Register of Deeds functions. Those who hold or claim interests in land may file documents with the Register of Deeds in an act that the statutes call *recording*.

The statutes may dictate the documents' form, such as that documents must bear signatures, be witnessed, and be notarized, and describe the lands adequately, perhaps by section number and by metes and bounds (that system of starting at a known point and measuring off distances in compass directions until arriving back at the starting point). Some of these provisions are to ensure the documents' reliability, while others are to ensure the documents' tracking. The Register of Deeds records the documents in such a way (formerly in large volumes while today much more so electronically) that a trained researcher can locate all documents having to do with a specific piece of land. The point of recording statutes is to ensure that anyone who researches and reads Register of Deeds records can track all claims on a certain piece of land, typically by using grantor-grantee and tract indexes, and plat maps.

Public notice of who owns or has an interest in land contributes importantly to the confidence that we have and need in the ready and reliable buying and selling (what lawyers call the *free alienation*) of land. The American economy would suffer if we did not have a reliable market for buying and selling land. Try buying property in countries without reliable recording systems, and you will recognize their value. In those other countries, it can take years to determine from whom one must buy, if one can at all determine the various primary and subsidiary interests. Would you buy land if you were unsure whether someone else other than person who was selling it to you already owned it? The American system of recording provides a way for sellers to ensure that they are getting that for which they pay, in legal terms, that they can search the chain of title to ensure good title. The system also reassures the banks or other financiers who will loan for the land's purchase or for building on it.

Of course, not all claims that people record about lands are genuine. Anyone can type up a deed, easement, mortgage, memorandum, lien, or other document and, by paying the modest fee that recording requires, record the document against a certain property. Doing so can instantly make the property unmarketable. Would you buy property to which someone else had already made a claim different than that which the seller believed genuine? In part because of the damage that recording a false claim can do against an owner and putative seller of property, state laws permit owners to maintain slander-of-title and other claims against false claimants.

So yes, you should probably record a document with the Register of Deeds notifying the public that you are buying this place on a land contract. You generally want to record your interest in land the moment that you acquire it. Because states adopt recording systems to warn and favor the diligent, state statutes tend to favor the first one to record an interest. Yes, some sellers are so nefarious as to sell the same interest to more than one buyer. Although the statutes vary in their design, in those cases the first buyer to record the interest may have the superior claim to the property simply because that buyer would have had less opportunity to learn of the other buyer's unrecorded interest.

Of course, you have other concerns when purchasing real property, whether by deed or land contract. Consult a lawyer about those other concerns. Your purchase may be one of the largest you will ever make. Get sound counsel so that you do not regret it.

22

Who's on First?

Question

I thought that I had heard of every kind of insurance — motor vehicle, homeowner's, life, health, disability, and so on. Then the real-estate agent with whom we listed our home started talking about title insurance. I don't remember buying title insurance when we bought the home. What's title insurance, and why do we need it?

Answer

Title insurance guarantees that what you own and, in this case, sell, is that for which your buyer pays. You need to procure the insurance because your buyer's bank or mortgage company won't lend without it. The lender must be sure that your buyer is getting that for which your buyer pays so that the lender has the mortgage security it requires. If you want to sell your home, then you have little or no choice in the matter. You will need to provide the insurance.

Title-insurance companies research the real-property records for the home that they are preparing to insure. They then issue a title commitment listing what their research discovered about who owns the home and who has various easements, mortgages, liens, or other interests in it. If you provide a valid deed meeting the title commitment's requirements, then the title-insurance company insures the title with the exceptions (easements, mortgages, etc.) that the title commitment lists. If the buyer and buyer's lawyer don't like those exceptions — if the buyer thought that the buyer was getting the home free and clear of the interests that the title research disclosed — then the buyer should exercise the title contingency in the purchase contract and walk away from the transaction unless you are able to cure the title defects.

While this process may sound complicated to you, it is a highly reliable way for buyers and their mortgage lenders to protect against title problems. Surprisingly strange things can happen with title to real property. Putative sellers may have forged signatures on prior deeds. Someone in the chain of title may have divorced, leaving a spouse with a dower or other interest in the land that buyers and sellers in the chain of title never quite managed to extinguish. Local government may have issued an assessment against the property for local road or utility improvements, or placed liens on the property for unpaid real-estate taxes. A utility or energy company may have an easement across the property. A homeowner's association may have placed architectural, use, or other restrictions on the property. A scrivener may have erred in the property description on a prior deed, leaving part of the land still in the hands of a prior seller.

Title companies take the risk of these kinds of problems when their research does not disclose them, their title commitment does not except them, and their title-insurance policies insure against those risks. The owner who suddenly discovers one of these problems with the owner's title can turn to the title-insurance company to hire a lawyer to fix the title problem. Failing a fix, the title company should pay for the loss, expense, and damage to the property's owner from the bad or clouded title.

You may not remember buying title insurance when you bought the home because you may not have paid for title insurance. In all likelihood, you do have title insurance relating to your purchase, particularly if you financed your purchase with a bank, which would very likely have required it. The seller probably paid for the title insurance. Conventions differ from locale to locale, but sellers typically carry certain of the closing costs, and title insurance is often one of those costs that sellers rather than buyers pay. After all, you should get that for which you pay, and title insurance is one way that the seller ensures that you do so.

Nothing is as simple as it looks. That adage applies as much to selling a home as it does to other large transactions. You and your buyer don't need loose ends in such an important transaction to both of you. The process of insuring title helps buyer and seller do their diligence around the transaction. The title insurance itself guarantees that any title issues are someone else's (the insurance company's) problem. Get the title insurance, and don't look back. You'll sleep better for it.

21

Signing on the Dotted Line

Question

I have a cousin who fell in love with a rich executive. Just before they married, he made her sign something they called a *prenup* and saying that she gets nothing if they divorce. So much for "until death do us part"! Are prenups legal?

Answer

Sometimes, in some places, depending on the disclosures.

Prenup is short for prenuptial agreement. The law sometimes calls a prenuptial agreement an *antenuptial agreement*, meaning an agreement signed ahead of or before the nuptials, referring to the marriage ceremony. Prenuptial agreements are exactly that, agreements that the marrying parties enter into to provide for their legal rights and financial interests during marriage and in the event of divorce. The agreements can be simple or complex, depending largely on the size and complexity of the financial interests held by one or the other party. When the marriage implicates substantial financial interests, the parties often involve

246

legal counsel to represent each party. Negotiations may ensue over the appropriate terms.

Prenuptial agreements are probably most common in two kinds of marriages. The one that most people think about is the marriage of a well-off person (often a business owner or entertainer) with substantial income and assets to a not-so-well-off person, perhaps beautiful or handsome and significantly younger. The disparity in financial resources raises concerns not the least of which is that the marriage is less about love or commitment than money. Blonde bombshell marries billionaire octogenarian. The other circumstance, less often recognized but possibly more common, is the second marriage of older equals. When divorced older persons of means remarry, the blending of families each of which already have adult children can raise concerns over inheritances. The first remarried spouse to die might (purposefully or not) leave everything to the other spouse and, soon enough, that other spouse's children, disinheriting the spouse's own children. Prenuptial agreements can be one way of keeping family finances separate while knitting together the relationships.

One problem that the law has long had with prenuptial agreements is that they anticipate divorce and thus may encourage or facilitate divorce. Society favors marriage. Making divorce easier by expecting and providing for divorce can frustrate the policy to promote marriage. Another problem that the law has had with prenuptial agreements is that they tend to be one sided. Sure, in some marriages involving a prenuptial agreement, both spouses bring substantial income and assets to the marriage so that relative bargaining strength is no concern. Yet in other marriages, one side has all the money and thus all or most of the bargaining power. The fiancé without money has no leverage other than love to strike a fair bargain. For these and related reasons, the law has long disfavored prenuptial agreements or treated them as suspect.

Yet as divorce rates increased and more states moved to no-fault divorce, states recognized prenuptial agreements as valid. State laws nonetheless tend to place restrictions on them. The parties must not have misrepresented their assets, and the agreement must not be coercive or unconscionable. If the richer party under-represents that party's riches, then the party will have induced the agreement by fraud, and the courts are likely to set aside the agreement. If the circumstances make it appear that the richer party coerced the poorer into signing away the last vestige of reasonable rights, then the courts may set aside the agreement as unconscionable. Given these limitations, parties entering into prenuptial agreements tend to accompany them with reasonably full disclosures of assets. The agreements also tend to make fair provision for the poorer spouse in the event of divorce rather than leaving the poorer spouse with nothing.

So, marriage in these cases may no longer be for richer or poorer, or in sickness and in health. Prenuptial agreements may seem like the devil's bargain. But in the right cases and done right, they can probably help. In complex cases, they may actually promote a healthy marriage. Here's hoping that's true for your cousin.

20 Your Fault, My Fault, Our Fault

Question

It seems to me that too few people these days are marrying and that too many people are divorcing. I keep hearing about *no-fault divorce*, making it as easy to end a marriage as to rent a new apartment or buy a new car. Can't the law make it harder to get a divorce?

Answer

We tried that, and it didn't really seem to work. Marriage is a legal, social, and sacramental union. As society changes in its attitude toward marriage, the law must also to some degree change. When the law tries to hold the line too severely against social trends, society finds a way around it.

Divorce law is state law and thus varies somewhat from state to state, but no-fault divorce is now routinely available. Traditionally, a spouse requesting a divorce had to show the court grounds for the divorce. Common grounds included the other spouse's adultery, cruelty (mental or physical abuse), desertion, or imprisonment. The divorcing spouse would plead one or more of those grounds and then offer testimony supporting the grounds, following which the court had the statutory authority to grant the divorce. The justification for fault-based divorce was that law should favor marriage and that marriages should persist unless grounds exist to terminate them. Yet doubtless, courts granted some divorces under these traditional laws even when none of the statutory grounds actually existed, on the false testimony of one or the other party.

The perjury of divorcing parties who made up grounds was one reason legislatures gave for adopting no-fault divorce. When spouses are ready to split, they will find a way (legal or not) to do so. You noticed that societal attitudes toward divorce have changed. Divorce no longer carries such social stigma with it. Law has recognized and accommodated that trend with no-fault divorce. A no-fault divorce is one in which the parties assert no grounds. The grounds may or may not exist. One or the other spouse may have been cruel or unfaithful. Yet the parties need not plead in a written complaint or testify in open court as to any particular grounds. Avoiding public disclosure of embarrassing grounds was another reason that legislatures had for adopting no-fault divorce.

Typically, in a no-fault divorce, all that the parties need to plead and prove is that they have irretrievably broken their marriage, and that they can no longer preserve it. A verified complaint will recite that breakdown language, and at least one of the parties will testify to it under oath in court. It only takes one spouse to divorce, even if the other spouse believes that they can save the marriage. In that sense, some divorced parties are truly blameless. They may have had little or no real responsibility for the marriage's breakdown and may strongly desire to see it persist. If, though, the other spouse wants to end it, then the other spouse can do so by meeting the statutory no-fault requirements. Those requirements typically do include a waiting period of some length (for example, 60 days in some states) between filing the complaint and receiving the final divorce judgment.

Some states, while recognizing no-fault divorce, still also recognize fault-based divorces. For religious or other reasons, some spouses would rather assert grounds for a divorce than pursue a no-fault divorce. Many marriages today still certainly have enough adultery and cruelty within them to find grounds for divorce. Indeed, whether the parties seek a no-fault or fault-based divorce, misconduct of one or both of the parties (particularly violence or other cruelty) can affect important issues like child custody, spousal support, and division of property. Read divorce pleadings and court papers, or watch divorce proceedings in court, and you will still see plenty of blame thrown back and forth even in no-fault divorces.

So, law cannot hold together what spouses wish to break apart. Promoting marriages and discouraging divorce takes more than just law. Culture, norms, social attitudes, and other influences have a lot to do with marriage and divorce rates. Don't expect law to do it for you. To a degree, we're all in this thing together.

19

What to Do with a Smoking Gun

Question

I saw on the news the other day that a murder suspect police had been pursuing turned himself in at his lawyer's office while still locked and loaded. Must have been an interesting day at the office. What do criminal-defense lawyers do when their clients provide them with evidence of the crime?

Answer

Take a deep breath, and then very carefully ensure that the evidence reaches law enforcement officials without the lawyer making an attorney-client disclosure or other breach of confidentiality.

You have asked a very good question, one that lawyers find difficult to address in some cases. The problem that lawyers face in receiving and handling evidence of crime is that they have two very clear duties that can conflict. One duty has to do with not concealing, tampering with, or destroying evidence of crime. A lawyer would not literally throw away the smoking gun. Yet even removing and securing a gun, knife, other weapon, or other

252

evidence of crime, somewhere other than where the lawyer found it, could easily constitute the destruction of evidence. Lawyers may not often visit crime scenes shortly after the crime and before police have inspected and secured it, but lawyers sometimes employ private detectives (often former police officers) to do so. When lawyers or their agents discover evidence, they must take care not to alter and in effect destroy it.

Yet for a lawyer representing a crime suspect, handling evidence is not as easy as promptly supplying it to the police or notifying police where to locate it, along with information about the suspect. Lawyers have duties to their clients. Those duties include not to disclose communications that fall within the attorney-client privilege and to maintain client confidentiality. If lawyers promptly informed police about anything their suspect clients said or provided, then suspects would not consult lawyers. Lawyers do not facilitate or cover up crime. Rather, suspects who consult lawyers routinely get sound counsel for the suspect to do the right thing, which may in cases include disclosure or even confession of the crime. We want suspects to consult lawyers, and so we protect their communications.

So when a suspect client brings the smoking gun or other weapon to a lawyer's office, or in some cases tells the lawyer where the suspect hid the crime weapon, the lawyer must find a way to get the weapon or information of its whereabouts to police authorities without disclosing the client's identity or communications. The lawyer may convey the weapon without any accompanying information or arrange for an intermediary to do so. In at least one jurisdiction, members of the local defense bar help one another out in making the weapon transfer or disclosure to police in a manner that keeps confidential the identity of the lawyer and client. The police get the weapon without getting the client's privileged communication or lawyer's confidential information. No such system is perfect, but it meets or comes close to meeting the policies behind the conflicting duties.

A related question has to do with the crime suspect. Lawyers have a duty not to harbor or conceal a fugitive from crime or otherwise aid in or assist a crime. The first advice that lawyers who counsel clients subject to arrest should give is to stop running and instead voluntarily turn himself or herself in to authorities. Running from arrest has its own hazards. Things go better, sometimes much better, for suspects who promptly submit to arrest. Bail, for instance, may be much more readily available when a suspect who learns of an arrest warrant promptly appears at the police station for the booking process. Standard counsel is to appear for booking immediately, although doing so make work best in the morning on a Tuesday or Wednesday to minimize the chance that the booked suspect will have to wait overnight or, worse, over a weekend for arraignment and release on bail.

Lawyers are representatives of their clients but also officers of the court. Lawyers owe both public and private duties. You should not find lawyers concealing evidence of crime. If a lawyer finds another lawyer concealing evidence, then the first lawyer must immediately report the second lawyer to bar officials. Law is an honorable and self-policing profession. You can and should trust lawyers, whether or not a suspect to crime.

18

Something Just Doesn't Look Right

Question

Our elementary school has a little guy who's always coming to school with bumps and bruises. Some of us parents suspect that things are not going so good for the boy at home. The bruises are too frequent and apparent, and the boy just seems to act as if someone has abused him. Aren't the teachers supposed to do something?

Answer

Yes, if they suspect or have reason to believe that someone has in fact abused the boy. You, too, can and should report your suspicion to the responsible officials.

While state laws can vary significantly on the specifics, states generally require schoolteachers and other professionals to report suspected child abuse to child-protective services. In some states, those reporting laws extend not just to schoolteachers but to physicians, nurses, social workers, daycare workers, and others who work with and around children. Some states even extend the duty to report to non-professionals like other parents in the child's school or neighborhood. Reporting statutes can have stiff penalties for the failure to report, including not just fines but jail time. Professionals take these obligations seriously. Those state laws on reporting child abuse may then require agencies receiving reports to cross-report among law enforcement, social-service agencies, and prosecutor's offices so that all entities having an interest in investigation and prosecution share the same information.

The standards that professionals must follow for reporting child abuse vary somewhat from state to state. A common standard requires that professionals must report any time that they suspect or have reason to believe that a child has suffered abuse or neglect. Frequent bruises, burns, or other marks where an adult might strike or otherwise abuse a child are obvious causes for report. Professionals must also report when they have knowledge of or actually observe conditions that would reasonably result in harm to the child. Teachers are less likely to observe such conditions, but social workers visiting a home might observe guns, drugs or drug-making equipment, and other hazardous conditions that would warrant report. Some states permit anonymous reports to the responsible agencies, but others require the reporting professional to identify him- or herself with contact information.

States also maintain citizen hotlines for reporting suspected child abuse. You can also report your concerns to the local child-protective-services agency or to police. If you do so, then keep your reports accurate and factual, and report only to the officials who have the authority to investigate. Do not spread rumors. Allegations of child abuse are serious and can severely harm a person's reputation. You likely have immunity under state defamation laws to report in good faith to state and local officials, even if your allegations turn out to be false. You lose that immunity when you know your reports are false or are reckless in your accusations, or if you spread rumors among persons who have no business in knowing. Child-abuse reporting laws also impose penalties for knowingly false reports. A frustrated or vengeful party in a fierce child-custody dispute may make a false allegation of child abuse in an effort to win custody, but doing so is extremely destructive and hazardous.

Schools can be the best place to discover child abuse. Teachers have substantial unsupervised interaction with children, who often learn to trust their teacher enough to reveal confidences that they would not to other professionals or adults. Schools also employ social workers, nurses, counselors, special-education professionals, and administrators, all of whom would have training in recognizing symptoms of child abuse. Coordinating information among these professionals can help identify or dispel concerns of child abuse. Collaboration can be key. Experts suspect that child abuse goes under-reported. Law gives observers every incentive and support to report and prevent child abuse. The abusers themselves of course face extremely stiff penalties. Parents who neglect or abuse their children face permanent loss of parental rights, criminal conviction, and imprisonment.

So, act responsibly, now. A child's life or safety may be at stake. Let child-protective officials do as they are trained to do. If nothing is wrong, then they can confirm so. Better safe than sorry.

17

Don't You Want to Be a Judge?

Question

I was in a courtroom the other day, and the thing that impressed me most was the way that everyone jumped when the judge said to. A few didn't look too happy about it, but the lawyers sure made a show of saying "Your Honor." Don't all lawyers want to be judges?

Answer

Not really, no. Certainly, judging has its moments. Judges do stand at or near the top of the profession. Yet the work can be unrelenting and the role exceedingly restrictive. Many lawyers are just fine with being lawyers and have no ambition to don the robes.

Judges without a doubt have the respect and admiration of the profession. That is in part why you heard lawyers using the traditional honorific. States and circumstances differ in how judges gain their bench. Many judges are elected. Some are first appointed and later elected or retained by election. Others presidents or governors appoint, federal judges on advice and

258

consent of the Senate, state judges sometimes with review and approval of state bar committees or judicial commissions. Once on the bench, judges serve independent of influence, except that they must comply with the constitutional or statutory grant of judicial authority and with a code of judicial ethics. Judges who misbehave face removal after tenure hearing.

Judging is critically important to communities. While we tend to look to appeals court judges as the movers and shakers of the legal world, local judges have significantly greater influence over the health, welfare, safety, order, character, and culture of a community. Every small judicial ruling has the capability of repairing (in the best case) or exacerbating (in the worst case) a tear in the community's fabric. Judges can redeem and heal, or they can further wound and insult. Of course, they tend very much to do the former rather than the latter. Courtrooms are generally places where law sets many small and large things, civil and criminal, individual and corporate, public and private, as right as they can be under difficult circumstances. Occasionally, things go especially well, and new opportunities arise out of what seemed like an unredeemable situation.

Lawyers, especially trial lawyers, know how difficult and isolating judging can be. Lawyers bring a matter to court, struggle with it, and return to the office to celebrate or lick their wounds. Judges struggle all day long with one court matter after another. Injustice never takes a day off. Holidays, spring breaks, and late-summer vacations all don't really matter. Cases keep coming. The matters themselves are too often horrific, especially the violent crimes, but also the wrongful deaths and serious personal injuries, and the child abuse and neglect, and the sexual misconduct, and the domestic violence, and the child-custody fights, and so on. You get the picture. Judging is seldom easy work. Humor barely enters into it. The few judges who are famously humorous or at least light-hearted tend in truth to use their humor to highlight deep pathos.

Judging is isolating in large part because of a judge's need to maintain strict independence from outside influence and to avoid even the appearance of bias. Conduct rules prohibit lawyers from speaking to judges about their cases outside of the presence of opposing counsel. While conventions differ from community to community, judges tend not to socialize with lawyers for that reason and to avoid the appearance of favoritism and bias. Judges eat lunch alone or with other judges. The professional and community relationships that they so enjoyed when in law practice fade away as their role prevents them from participating not just in cases but also in causes and on boards and in fundraising. Lawyers have none of these restrictions.

The hardest part of the judicial role may be internal. Judges must know and temper the influence on themselves of their own judicial authority. Judges are never wrong in their own courtroom. Everyone does or should do just what the judge says. Yet judges must maintain a reasonable humility. Lawyers find themselves constantly humbled by their opponents and even their own clients. The challenge for a lawyer is to maintain the lawyer's confidence. The challenge for a judge is to temper the judge's confidence, to recognize that their authority is only delegated from a higher source. No, not all lawyers want to be judges. And not all lawyers should be judges. Only some lawyers have sound judicial character and temperament.

16

Hair Today, Gone Tomorrow

Question

I keep encouraging a friend of mine who has been doing my hair to start a business with it, but she says she doesn't have the schooling or the license. Do you really have to have a license just to cut someone's hair?! Seems like you have to have a license to do just about anything these days, like eat, sleep, and breathe.

Answer

Yes, you have to have a license for hair-cutting businesses. Cutting hair involves just enough of a public-health issue that states in their power to regulate general commerce feel that some training and licensure is necessary. You know, things like head lice. You wouldn't want them, and yet cut hair in unsanitary way and you just might end up with them or other disease issues.

Cosmetology and barber schools do deal with public-health issues. Of course, they also deal with hairstyles, hair products, other dimensions of beauty and personal aesthetics, customer-relationship management, and many other things necessary or helpful to running a personal-services business. The schools vary in their missions and qualities. Some schools are for-profit entities organized around a product brand. Other schools have different focuses. They all help students satisfy state requirements for licensure or certification. Those requirements, while differing state to state, can include a certain number of classroom or apprenticeship hours plus passing a board exam. Even once an examinee passes, the state may require continuing education and periodic license or certification renewal. States may offer (or require) multiple licenses for which cosmetology schools will train, not just the basic barbering or hairstyling licenses but licenses or certifications as an esthetician or for hair braiding. The schools may also train in manicure, pedicure, massage, and other arts.

Of course, cosmetology is not the state regulator's sole interest. Consider the trades, whether electrical, plumbing, heating and cooling, and so on. The traditional professions like medicine, nursing, accounting, and law have their own regulators, sometimes similar in constitution to other administrative boards, but in the case of law distinct. Lawyers regulate their own. Professions to an extent embrace their own regulation in that it certifies to the public their value, making them marketable and distinct while also limiting their numbers and thus competition within the profession. Protection of the public, though, is the pattern. Librarians, who certainly have professional education and memberships, have no state-required licensure, while morticians do. Grocery-store clerks don't, while daycare operators do. Artists don't, while exterminators do. You see the public-protection pattern, although other professions represent close calls. States also require fishing and hunting guides and taxidermists to obtain licenses.

States regulate professions largely through administrative powers. The state legislature will determine whether a certain profession requires regulation for public health and safety. If so, then the state legislature will typically enact a statute or code highlighting the regulatory concerns in broad outline while simultaneously creating or empowering an administrative board or agency to promulgate and enforce detailed regulations. The regulations will set forth the requirements for the license. State legislatures have modest staffs and budgets. State administrative agencies, codes, staffs, and budgets can in relative terms be vast. It takes a lot to regulate a profession.

Lawyers by the way assist license applicants whom state officials unfairly deny. As your concern indicates, we do have a basic liberty to work in our chosen field or profession. While the state may place reasonable restrictions on that choice, it must not deny the right arbitrarily or capriciously. The state must also provide applicants with due-process rights to notice and hearing. If the state denies or removes a license unfairly, then get the help of a lawyer with expertise in administrative hearings. One misplaced complaint from a demented nursing-home resident could cost a devoted aide her state license, ability to work in her only qualified field, and sole means of support. An administrative hearing may correct the error. Licensure can be serious business.

Oh, and on a license to eat, sleep or breathe? Don't worry, and don't hold your breath.

15

Bond, But Not James Bond

Question

On our local public-access cable-television channel, I am always hearing about the various public boards discuss bond authorities and bond issues. The only bond I know is James Bond, but somehow I don't think that they're talking about 007. What is a bond authority?

Answer

A bond authority is a governmental unit that raises capital for a public project by issuing debt in the form of securities that private or institutional investors can buy to earn interest often exempt from at least some taxes. The authority issues bonds at a certain interest rate for a certain duration. Investors, whether individuals or institutions like pensions and other investment funds, buy the bonds to guarantee the percentage return that the interest-rate promises until the bond matures, at which point the investor would receive back the amount of the bond. Investors may also trade the bonds (buy and sell the bonds) with their value increasing or decreasing depending on how their interest rate compares to current interest rates for new bond issues.

While the concept of a bond authority is complex, the purpose is simple: to raise money. Government is just like individuals and private corporations in that government often wants to acquire something before it can afford to pay for it. Borrowing is one way to do so. Private corporations borrow from banks. They also occasionally issue private corporate bonds, which operate like public bonds issued by a governmental unit such as a bond authority. When governmental units issue public bonds, earnings from the public bonds are often tax free at the federal, state, or local level depending on the issuer. The tax-free status of some public bonds gives them an advantage over stock shares, private corporate bonds, and other taxable investments.

Authority bonds, very similar to *municipal bonds* or *munis,* are often thought to have an additional advantage of being secure as investments. Investors presume security in part from the fact that the issuer is government, and government is supposed to be credible. Yet bond authorities or other governmental units issuing bonds may also back the bonds with something specific such as tax or other revenue from the public asset that the authority hopes to develop or support with the money raised by the bond issue. A bond authority might issue bonds to build a bridge, for instance, and then pledge toll revenue from the bridge specifically to ensure that the investors get their interest and bonds paid. While bonds have traditionally been secure investments, recent city and county bankruptcies, and high levels of debt in certain states, have perhaps proven that no investment is perfectly secure.

Government units use bonds to build not only bridges but schools, hospitals, sports arenas, convention centers, performance halls, courthouses, sewers and other public utilities, and other public projects. The professional services of bond lawyers are obviously critical in bringing together the multiple project participants that bond issues require, not only investors and the governmental unit but also banks, local, state, and federal officials, construction companies, and community representatives. Just as lawyers are critical to bond issues, so too is law critical to bond authorities. Federal, state, and local laws may all grant or otherwise affect the ability of a bond authority to issue bonds, particularly if the bonds are to qualify as exempt from income taxes. Securities laws also heavily regulate the offering of bonds.

While the public-access-television bond discussions that you see are probably not your favorite television show, public finance is fascinating and important. Ask a bond lawyer. They love what they do.

14

What's Native About a Casino?

Question

I just don't get it. Indian tribes own and run all the casinos in our area, and the casinos are right downtown, not on some distant reservation. What is it about Native-American tribes and casinos? Tribes don't own the casinos in Vegas.

Answer

The prevalence of Indian casinos, or if you prefer, Native American gaming, is an unusual creature of sovereignty, law, and opportunity.

Traditionally, most American states have disfavored, indeed outlawed, casino gambling. The well-known and longstanding exceptions have been Atlantic City in New Jersey and Las Vegas. But major portions of the U.S. population live a long way from both of those gambling meccas. Indian casinos have filled that vacuum. Because of claims of Native-American sovereignty, Indian casinos are able to operate on reservations in states where casino gambling is illegal or sharply limited. Once recognized by the federal government, Native-American tribes may establish the laws that they wish to establish on their reservations, which are sovereign territory, even when those laws conflict with the laws of the U.S. state in which the reservation is located. If a tribe wishes to permit casino gambling on its reservation, then it may generally do so, under federal law that grants states only limited powers.

So how does a Native-American tribe get to operate a casino downtown? With federal approval, a tribe may reach a compact with a state to take land into the tribe's reservation. That land does not have to be undeveloped lands far from population centers. The state may form a compact with a tribe for the tribe to occupy downtown lots and buildings as reservation land. The downtown-reservation concept may not be as far-fetched or artificial as you may think. Native Americans may well have occupied that downtown land long before it became a metropolitan center. But federal law imposes no such limit in any case. Federal government approval is the key because the federal government, not the state, is the sovereign with which the tribe, also a sovereign, meets. The state actually has less say in the arrangement than one might think. As long as the federal government approves, the state and tribe may form a compact to locate the reservation where a casino makes economic sense.

And economics is where the opportunity part comes in. Native Americans do not operate casinos out of any particular cultural heritage. Rather, the dearth of casinos in states where casino gambling is illegal or severely restricted just makes running a casino too attractive for many tribes (though not nearly all—fewer than half of tribes run casinos) to pass up. Unless reservation lands have substantial natural resources like oil and gas, the tribe may have very little economic opportunity. Its members may lack education, vocational skills, transportation, and other building blocks for an economically successful life. Casinos can generate substantial revenue for their owners, even when others manage the casinos. Some tribes also use the casino business to train and employ their members, adding to the economic benefit flowing from the casino's earnings.

Not every Indian casino is a gold-mine operation. Indian casinos have had more and more competition both among themselves and from riverboat gambling, racetrack gambling, online gambling, state lotteries, and other forms of legalized gaming. The public, or at least state legislatures, embrace less heartily the traditional objections to gambling, that it robs, addicts, and demoralizes. While gambling once corrupted, gaming is entertainment, even good family fun for some, or so more and more seem to feel. These changes in attitudes and then in gaming laws may mean that Indian casinos will soon lose most or all of their remaining legal advantage. Whether they survive may simply depend on whether their head start enabled them to build superior gaming businesses.

13

The Character to Practice Law

Question

I know a lawyer who got arrested recently for drunk driving. Now that's got to be something to behold, a lawyer hauled into court for breaking the law. What happens to lawyers who break the law?

Answer

For starters, the same thing that happens to anyone else. Lawyers get no pass for drunk driving or any other law breaking. Indeed, lawyers who do not obey the law may also face character-and-fitness challenges to their licensure. Lawyers can lose their privilege to practice law simply because they break the law even when they do so unrelated to their law practice.

Lawyers practice law under professional-conduct rules that grievance commissions enforce. If a lawyer does something wrong related to law practice, like knowingly offering false testimony or charging an exorbitant fee, then grievance administrators may suspend or revoke the lawyer's license, putting the lawyer out of practice. Yet sometimes, a lawyer will

270

do something wrong that has nothing directly to do with law practice, like drunk driving or assault and battery in a bar fight. The question then becomes whether the wrong should affect the lawyer's privilege to practice law. Just because a lawyer gets in a bar fight, does that mean that the lawyer should not be able to practice law to make a living?

The law governing lawyers answers that question by including in the professional-conduct rules a provision that makes anything that demonstrates the lawyer's substantial unfitness to practice law a violation of the rules. That rule is a catch-all provision for the odd crimes that a lawyer might commit completely outside of his or her law practice but that nonetheless suggests that the lawyer could harm a client while practicing law. Would you want a lawyer who intentionally wrote bad checks or maybe shoplifted in his or her personal life? Very probably not because that conduct suggests a character issue that could lead the lawyer to write you a bad check or steal something of yours that you entrusted to the lawyer. Someone who works in the skilled trades or in manufacturing might present no particular risk to anyone at work for having written bad checks or shoplifted. Yet lawyers occupy such positions of trust as to require good character and the fitness to practice law.

A certain recent former U.S. president who happened also to be a licensed lawyer is an example. State bar officials concluded that the president had purposefully testified falsely while under oath in a deposition in a civil case. The president was not practicing law at the time. His act of bad character happened to be in his own civil case. His falsehood may have hurt no one directly, at least not financially. Yet state bar officials decided to revoke the president's law license presumably because of the risk that bad character created of harm to future clients. When character issues arise, state bar officials empanel other lawyers to hear evidence and determine whether the charged conduct occurred and, if so, whether the conduct demonstrated substantial unfitness to practice law.

Drunk driving may be one of the harder calls to make for character-and-fitness panels. Some might conclude that while drunk driving presents substantial risk to others using the public highway, it presents little or no risk to clients who might later retain the sobered-up lawyer. On the other hand, drunk driving indicates a serious disregard for the law. Lawyers cannot be effective advocates for justice while simultaneously flouting the law in their personal lives, particularly with conduct as dangerous as drunk driving. Drunk driving can also indicate a serious substance-abuse problem, when substance abuse can indicate a lack of self-control, depression, or other mental or emotional-health problems. While state bars have lawyer-assistance programs to help prevent and overcome substance abuse, character-and-fitness panels take the issue seriously.

Character-and-fitness panels regularly have to make these difficult judgments about what to do with a lawyer who breaks the law. A doctor can be pretty unhealthy and still be a good doctor. A good dentist can have bad teeth. But a lawyer who breaks the law with impunity most likely cannot make a good lawyer. While a scoundrel lawyer may not get caught immediately, the profession polices itself quite effectively, requiring lawyers to report on one another or suffer discipline themselves. You can trust that licensed lawyers have the decent character to practice law.

12

Licensing Liquor

Question

I read in the local paper the other day about a local convenience store that may lose its license to sell liquor because of a sting operation the police did with involving illegal sales to minors. Why does the law regulate liquor sales?

Answer

A combination of history, epidemiology, and economy. The 1920s prohibition era lay the groundwork for state and federal regulators. Once the nation and individual states began legalizing alcohol sales again, the public expected or accepted close regulation. For as long as humankind has been ingesting the stuff, alcohol has caused public-health problems that regulation continue to address. And both the states that regulate and tax alcohol distribution and sales, and the bars and retail stores that profit from its restricted sale, have economic interests in its continued regulation. Given this mix of circumstances, don't expect to see widespread deregulation soon.

273

Amendments to the U.S. Constitution, first to prohibit alcohol sales and then to permit them, marked the Prohibition Era. Public opposition to drinking, marked by temperance societies that gained substantial political influence, grew to the point that the required supermajority of states approved the amendment to ban sales. Prohibition spawned a backlash that included a culture of disrespect for the law. Law enforcement was ineffective in countering, and sometimes coopted by, the criminal activity supporting illegal liquor sales. The nation's mood swung quickly to the point of believing that close regulation was better than absolute prohibition. Law has a hard time banning what the public knows it should not do but is going to do anyway.

Both federal and state laws regulate liquor sales. The federal Bureau of Alcohol, Tobacco, Firearms and Explosives (known as ATF — explosives are a recent addition to the Bureau's mission), an agency within the U.S. Department of Justice, investigates illegal diversion and interstate distribution of alcohol, while states maintain liquor-control commissions that license bars, restaurants, and retailers. Licensing limited numbers of sellers enables the state to hold sellers responsible for violating regulations prohibiting sales to minors and the visibly intoxicated. It also helps ensure that those sellers carry insurance against the loss that illegal sales can cause. Licensing also limits competition among sellers, creating a market for the licenses themselves. States tax alcohol sales, raising revenue not only for enforcement but for general funds and other programs. Given the revenue boost, the electorate accepts state involvement in alcohol distribution and sales, just as the public in many states permit the state to run lotteries while outlawing or limiting private lotteries and other gambling.

The epidemiology of alcohol obviously has to do in part with rank drunkenness. Drunkenness carries costs at home in the form of domestic violence and child abuse and neglect, at work in the form of absenteeism and inattention to safety and productivity, and publicly in the form of death and serious injury from drunk

274

driving and violence or disruption from public intoxication. Federal and state laws recognize these harms and deal with them both directly and indirectly. Drunk driving is a serious crime the penalties for which continue to increase. Selling or furnishing alcohol to minors is likewise a crime. Alcohol addiction is a serious problem to which the young are peculiarly prone. Tens of thousands of Americans die each year from binge drinking, many of them youths. About twice as many Americans die of binge drinking as from motor-vehicle accidents, when those accidents cause well over 30,000 deaths each year. Public-health officials estimate that binge drinking alone costs the U.S. economy a couple of hundred *billion* dollars each year.

The law has plenty of reason to regulate alcohol sales. Don't expect regulations to relax, especially as public-health officials continue to document the social and economic harms that flow from over-consumption of alcohol.

11

An Unlikely Suspect

Question

The airport security screener took my wife behind a curtain to search her clothing for a bomb. My wife is the least scary looking person on earth. Don't we have a constitutional right against unreasonable searches?

Answer

Yes, but reasonableness permits searches, not just profiled searches but random searches, when it comes to air-traffic security. Think 9-11.

The constitutional protection about which you speak is the Fourth Amendment's prohibition on unreasonable searches and seizures. Government officials must not search private citizens unreasonably. We usually think of the Fourth Amendment as having to do with the investigation of crime, where police officers must have probable cause to arrest and search. Yet your intuition is correct that the Fourth Amendment also applies to public-security searches to prevent crime and for public safety. Roadway sobriety check lanes are an example. The Fourth Amendment governs police officers who try to prevent drunk driving and catch drunk drivers in random check-lane stops. Likewise, the federal Transportation Security Administration (or TSA as we know it) is a government agency. The Fourth Amendment governs the conduct of security officers who search travelers at the airport. The TSA protects the security of travelers in order to uphold the Constitution and laws of the United States, not to violate the Constitution and break the laws.

The Fourth Amendment nonetheless permits both profile and random searches at airports because of the peculiarly significant security concerns having to do with air travelers. We expect searching before boarding an airliner, indeed hoping that the searches are effective. We thus have less of a sense of privacy, making searches more reasonable. By contrast, we might well not expect a TSA search at a bus, subway, or railroad station. The hazards of air travel are quite different and significantly more acute than the hazards of land travel. Although it does have programs operating outside of airports, the TSA may have significantly less constitutional authority to perform searches, particularly random searches, at those other locations, depending on the circumstances and risks of travel.

Profiling, while controversial and often unlawful when done by race, religion, or other protected categories, is nonetheless a common security practice and useful security tool. Where the passenger has traveled and how the passenger acts, for instance, can give clues to suspect intentions and behaviors. The TSA, which is an agency within the U.S. Department of Homeland Security, maintains a watch-list database that helps identify individuals who may present security risks. Travelers who find themselves stopped and searched frequently may have inaccurate information or be misidentified in the TSA's database and can review and challenge that information.

Your wife, though, was likely subject to a random search, not a profile search. Profiling is not sufficient. Terrorists have recruited women and children, young and old, and even the mentally disabled to carry explosive devices. The risks of concealment are not simply in the carry-on handbags, backpacks, and laptop computers. Terrorists have designed and attempted to use shoe bombs, underwear bombs, and other explosive devices sewn into clothing. These challenges make more-invasive searches reasonable under the Fourth Amendment's standard. The TSA continues to develop and deploy different tools and methods including body scans and clothing searches.

The TSA's increasingly thorough methods do create new risks of abuse. The information about you that the TSA collects could pose a risk to you or your finances if not maintained securely. The law requires the TSA to hold that information most securely. TSA officers have access to personal property including wallets and purses containing cash and valuables, and jewelry. The TSA operates sting programs to ensure that its officers do not steal personal property. The law also protects you against unreasonable searches. TSA security officers who misuse searches or search images or results for personal interests face administrative sanction. Federal law also creates private rights of action for damages for these constitutional violations.

If you suspect abuse of the TSA's search mission, then report the matter to the TSA's inquiry program, and consult a lawyer with expertise in civil-rights matters. We need security in air travel, but abuses of security measures do happen. Keep the system honest while respecting the importance of its function. Arrive a little earlier and prepare for some degree of search. And then hope that you or your wife do not get the random-search treatment.

10

Laws of War

Question

Recently, I have seen in the news some of the most ghastly atrocities committed by warring forces including gassing, kidnappings, rape, mass executions, genocide, and beheadings. I thought that we had laws of war. What is happening?

Answer

Nations do recognize laws of war through conventions and treaties. The problem is that the fighting forces may have no particular allegiance to any nation or, if they do, then to their laws, conventions, and treaties. Nations may through international courts hold leaders of those forces responsible in war-crime tribunals following the capture of those leaders, as was the case with the Nuremberg trials of Nazi leaders following World War II and as has been the case involving leaders of more-recent genocides. But the war involving those forces may well still be lawless. When nations war, we have some small hope of some degree of honor in the conduct of battle, although history is replete with lawless actions sanctioned at least tacitly by national

279

leaders. Yet when fighting forces have little or no recognized political structure, the prospect for accountability to laws of war diminishes to the point of zero.

The very concept of laws of war is fraught with tension. War happens when law, or the system of adjusting national rights and interests, fails. War is power, not authority. Yet the atrocities of war led nations to establish ground rules followed at least some of the time by some nations. The Geneva Convention, which is a collection of treaties and protocols, is the most-cited example. The Convention nations meant to protect non-combatants against the atrocities of war. For instance, military members should identify themselves by uniform to distinguish them from opposing forces and from civilians. We know, though, that some fighting forces deliberately wear the uniform of the opposition in order to infiltrate the opposition or deliberately dress like and hide among civilians. Fighting forces may hide bombs and other weapons in schools and hide themselves in or even actively fight from religious sanctuaries simultaneously occupied by non-combatants.

Some forces simply break one protocol after another. They may in doing so gain temporary military advantage. They may also so thoroughly demonstrate their depravity that the civilized world takes notice and unifies in arms against them. The history of war may be that, while war itself seems atrocious for the loss of life and destruction that it brings even to the non-combatant, individual acts of atrocity within war lead slowly but inevitably to judgment. After all, what population can support a fighting force that transgresses every last moral convention? Terror organizations by definition fight to strike fear in the hearts of non-combatants. Yet fear is itself a sufficient motivator to turn against the organizations and causes that propagate it. Humankind lives under the call of liberty, a call for which we have demonstrated that we will fight and fight again, to the end.

Wars have always had customs, since ancient times. In modern times, and with the help of many lawyers, nations have shaped those customs into international conventions that we know as the law of war. The public may not fully appreciate it, but lawyers play a role in war, helping generals and other military leaders understand and follow the laws of war while sometimes also helping military leaders develop rules of engagement. Rules of engagement tell military members when they may use force, for instance in self-defense or to return hostile fire, and when they must not use force, such as to seize territory or personal property, or detain civilians. Wise and responsible military leaders abide by the laws of war and rules of engagement, even when in the short term doing so may appear to create military disadvantage. Law has a role in war just as in peace.

9

Objection! Hearsay!

Question

A friend of mine and I were having a friendly argument when, all of a sudden, my friend objected that I was relying on *hearsay*. I told my friend that he's not a lawyer and didn't know what he was talking about. But neither did I know. What is hearsay?

Answer

To lawyers, hearsay is the rule of evidence that prohibits a witness from testifying in court to what another person said out of court, in order to prove the truth of what that other person said. When non-lawyer members of the public use the same term, they mean something very like the same definition, although lawyers know how precise and tricky hearsay's definition can be.

Courts decide cases on testimony from witnesses and on documents and other exhibits admitted into evidence. In theory, judges admit testimony and exhibits into evidence only when the rules of evidence, of which we have both state and federal, authorize the admission. In practice, some evidence inevitably makes its way into evidence without the rules' authorization, perhaps because one of the lawyers is asleep at the proverbial wheel or tactically has no reason to object to it. Your friend could have just ignored your hearsay rather than objecting. Just because a judge admits evidence does not mean that the judge or jury must give it weight or credence when deciding. Much hearsay, for instance, makes its way into evidence through one or more of the many hearsay exceptions. Nothing says that a judge or jury must trust or believe the admitted hearsay.

Lawyers receive substantial training in the rules of evidence. Rules of evidence are primarily a way of ensuring that the information on which judges and juries decide cases is reliable. Relevance, for example, is an evidence rule that ensures that judges and juries hear only things that should actually make a difference to the outcome. A related rule, though, prohibits relevant evidence that is nonetheless unduly prejudicial. Just because something is relevant does not mean that the judge or jury should hear it. The unfair way in which it colors a claim or party may outweigh its small probative value. For example, in a personal-injury case involving a motor-vehicle striking a pedestrian in the crosswalk, the fact that the pedestrian is an occasional substance abuser could arguably be relevant to the pedestrian's claim for loss of future earnings. Drug users may statistically make less in earnings. But juries might well place far too much weight on that barely probative evidence, punishing the pedestrian for the drug use rather than compensating the pedestrian fairly for the injury.

So what is the problem with hearsay that the rules of evidence exclude much of it (except for the exceptions)? When an in-court witness testifies to what an out-of-court person said previously, we have to ask why not just have the out-of-court person testify to it in court, where the person would be under oath, under penalty of perjury, and subject to cross-examination? We can rely much more confidently on in-court witnesses than out-of-court statements, so we exclude many out-of-court statements. We do not exclude every out-of-court statement, though. We only exclude out-of-court statements that the in-court proponent tries to use to prove the truth of the out-of-court statement. "The traffic light was red" would be classic hearsay in a case involving a claim of negligence for running a red light because the eyewitness's statement is exactly what the claimant hopes to prove in court. The claimant must call the eyewitness to trial to testify in court to that same observation. By contrast, eyewitness statements that the victim cried in pain at the scene would not be hearsay because not used to prove anything that the actual cries asserted.

Lost you already? And we hadn't even gotten to the couple of dozen exceptions to the hearsay rule, for things like business records, admissions by a party opponent, excited utterances, operative language, present-sense impressions, and so on. Evidence rules are a fascinating study in the vagaries of observation, recall, and proof of events and circumstances. Trial lawyers give a lot of attention to evidence rules. Now you know a bit more about why law school is such a valuable intellectual challenge. Respect and rely on your lawyer, especially when it comes to evidence. Law is a science as well as an art.

8

Your Right, My Right, Copyright

Question

Years ago, I had a great idea for a book, film, or television show. Recently, I saw a trailer for a movie that looks exactly like my idea. I presume that it is too late this time, but how does one go about copyrighting an idea so that others cannot steal it?

Answer

One does not copyright ideas. The copyright laws protect original works of authorship fixed in a tangible means of expression. Next time, write down your idea.

Copyright law is federal law, grounded in the U.S. Constitution and supported by statutory enactment. Congress enacted and periodically amends copyright laws to promote writings, music, art, and other expression. Just as you intuit, copyright enables the authors and owners of intellectual works to control and profit from those works particularly when others value them. Copyright is only set of laws that protect intellectual property. Patents involve another set of laws addressing protection of inventions. Trademark law and trade secret law are other forms of intellectual-property law that enable individuals and entities to own, control, and protect images and other marks associated with their interests.

You are also correct that copyright law is a primary means by which creators and owners of television shows and films prevent theft and control distribution. You have certainly heard of unauthorized websites uploading shows and films, and of internet users downloading and viewing or even selling them. The copyright laws provide powerful enforcement mechanisms to prevent those and other forms of theft. Copyright holders can win damages and even punitive damages against violators while also obtaining court injunctions to shut down websites and prevent further violations. Some of the famous (for artists, we should say infamous) commercial file-sharing websites like the original Napster fell victim to copyright laws.

The copyright laws often confuse creators of copyrightable material. You need not publish your work in order for you to own the copyright in it. Copyright also protects unpublished works as long as you fix them in a tangible form of expression. You also need not register a work in order to own the copyright in it. You own the copyright in it as soon as you fix your idea in a tangible form of expression. Registration is another way of alerting the world to your ownership while also facilitating your ability to enforce your copyright. With registration, you could win statutory damages and attorney's fees. You also need no longer put a copyright notice (the word or symbol followed by the year and your name) on everything that you wish to protect. If you wish to alert others that you intend to protect your expression, then go ahead and put a copyright notice on it, although such notices are no longer necessary for newer works.

You may in the future have other ways to protect an idea, at least if you disclose it to creative types who turn it into a commercial product. People who form concepts for what could turn into hit shows or films can share those concepts under confidentiality agreements that prohibit the producers from using

286

the idea without permission. Inventors sometimes do the same, disclosing their idea for an invention before obtaining or applying for a patent but only under an agreement that prevents the designer or manufacturer to whom they disclose it from using it without permission. So if you don't want to write the script for your next idea, and would rather disclose it to someone who could, then consider forming an agreement with them that lets you control the use of your idea. Consult a lawyer with expertise in intellectual-property matters.

7

The Next Big Thing

Question

I'd been spending a lot of time in my garage and basement tinkering with things when the idea hit me. It only took a few years and a couple hundred thousand dollars to develop a prototype. My invention is ready for manufacture, but I don't want anyone stealing it when I am sure that I've invented the next big thing. What do I do for protection?

Answer

Patent your next big thing.

Congress intends patent law to spur inventions by making ownership rights available to inventors. Inventors deserve and indeed require a return on their investments particularly if they, like you, devote substantial time and resources to their inventions. Inventors and those who finance them should have property or other rights in the income stream that the inventions may produce if the inventors are going to continue inventing and the financiers continue financing the inventions. Major design firms and manufacturers in all fields including transportation, electronics, software, biotechnology, medical devices, drugs, and so on depend heavily on patents. Manufacturers may own or license thousands of patents in complex portfolios that they manage to preserve their economic advantage and interests.

Patents cover new and useful machines, processes, manufactured articles, and compositions of matter, or improvements to any of those things. They also cover ornamental designs for manufactured articles. Patent law's requirement that your invention be new is important. You may never have seen someone else's identical design when you dreamed up your own invention, but if it already existed within the state of the relevant art, then you will likely not get a patent. Patent law's requirement that your invention be useful means that it must provide some identifiable benefit to its user. One may see many hare-brained inventions patented, but unless they were only of the ornamental-design type, they had at least a reasonable argument for some degree of utility.

You apply for a patent with the U.S. Patent and Trademark Office. Simply because you apply does not mean that you will be successful. Patents differ from copyright in that respect. Patent examiners working for the Patent Office examine the invention's description, compare it to inventions already patented, and reject applications that do not meet patent law's requirements. While many inventors grow sophisticated in the search and description skills that successful patent applications generally require, many more benefit from a patent lawyer's representation. Lawyers must obtain an additional license, earned by successful examination, to practice before the Patent Office and courts. That license and the special expertise that patent work requires encourages lawyers to specialize in patent work.

Patents do not absolutely prevent others from mimicking designs. In fact, the quid pro quo for patent protection is your disclosure of the invention. You must file publicly detailed drawings and explanations describing your invention, from which dishonest manufacturers could reproduce your invention. Other

289

manufacturers can also reverse engineer products to discover unique designs. Knock-off products are widespread globally. While other nations may recognize U.S. patents, enforcement especially against foreign manufacturers can be problematic. Enforcement, though, can also be effective, especially domestically. Patent holders have strong legal protections including not only civil damage claims that can include statutory damages and fee awards but also court injunctions. If someone wants to participate in making and marketing your patented product, then it should license that right from you.

Short of patenting, you may be able to contract with a manufacturer to review your prototype and design confidentially for it to determine whether it will assist you with a patent application or other exploitation of your invention. You don't absolutely have to patent first, although doing so can make very good sense. Consult with a lawyer who has intellectual-property expertise. If you've invented the next big thing, then you had better get going with it before someone beats you to market.

6

Junk Science in the Courtroom

Question

Every time I read, see, or hear an account of a trial, some big shot with a lot of letters after his or her name is claiming to be an expert witness in some weird science. It all seems a little suspicious to me. Where do lawyers find these guys, and is there really anything to their opinions?

Answer

The courts have learned to jealously guard against junk science in the courtroom. Most courts carefully ensure that any witness whom a party claims to be an expert on some issue that the court will decide, first meets several requirements ensuring that their opinions have a scientific basis. The day of the charlatan expert, if it ever existed, is largely over.

Federal and state rules of evidence empower the trial court to determine who may or must not testify. We usually think of a witness as someone who observed some important event, like a bystander eyewitness to a crime or motor-vehicle accident. Lawyers call them *fact witnesses*. Yet the rules of evidence also contemplate that parties may retain *expert witnesses* to testify at trial. Expert witnesses have no particular knowledge of the facts other than what fact witnesses report or documents or exhibits establish. Indeed, the first thing that a lawyer will do after identifying and retaining the right expert is to provide the expert with the factual record on which the expert will form opinions and testify. While that role may sound a lot like what the judge or jury should do, that is, evaluate the factual evidence, the rules of evidence permit parties to retain and offer the testimony of experts when the issue that the judge or jury must decide requires peculiar knowledge.

Expert witnesses are common, indeed required, in medical and other malpractice cases, for instance. If you were not a physician, then would you know what a physician should have done under a certain circumstance? Or if the case is one of accounting malpractice or engineering malpractice, would you have known what an accountant or engineer should have done? Parties in those cases instead retain expert physicians, accountants, and engineers to testify to the professional standard of care. Many other cases, though, can also require expert witnesses. Physicians testify in personal-injury cases as to how bad the injuries are and whether they are likely to heal. Vocational experts testify whether a claimant can or cannot work. Labor economists testify as to lost wages. Toxicology experts testify as to blood-alcohol levels and their probable effects. Coroners testify as to cause of death. The list goes on and on.

These examples probably sound non-controversial, but controversy can readily attend expert testimony. Sometimes, experts attempt to testify out of their field such as when a physician in one specialty criticizes a physician in another specialty, or a mechanical engineer testifies to what a chemical engineer would know. Other times, the expert attempts to testify in such a narrow or peculiar field that we may wonder whether the field truly represents a body of expert knowledge, like a slip-and-fall expert, or a snow-and-ice-removal expert, or an expert in mother-daughter relationships. Experts earn Ph.D. degrees in many peculiar fields not all of which would the courts recognize.

While the law of experts varies somewhat from state to state, federal trial courts and many state trial courts apply a standard that the U.S. Supreme Court articulated. That standard requires the expert to address whether other experts have tested the theory behind the expert's opinion, the expert or others have published the theory subject to peer review, the theory is often or seldom erroneous, the theory produces measurable standards, and the relevant community of experts has accepted the theory. The trial courts will often first hold a hearing at which the expert must establish the validity and reliability of the expert opinions under this standard before the trial judge admits it into evidence at a subsequent trial. This rigorous standard and procedure for admitting expert testimony eliminates most or all of the feared junk science.

Experts can influence trial outcomes. They are sometimes, maybe often, the showmen at trial, knowing more than anything how to testify clearly and convincingly. Yet they must nonetheless be credible in their expertise. The law assures it.

5

Wordsmithing

Question

It was kind of funny. When the meeting was nearly over, and it was time to write up the recommendations, we all turned to the lawyer in the group to do it for us. What makes lawyers so persnickety and so good at writing?

Answer

They do a lot of it when it is important. Lawyers are not necessarily born writers. Many are made writers. But most are good writers, and some are outstanding writers.

Law schools of course teach legal writing. Legal writing, though, may not be what you think. Law schools tend not to teach law students any or much Latin, for instance. Indeed, the professional trend for many years has been the opposite, to help law students and lawyers learn to write in plain English while also writing precisely. Lawyers have learned to eschew the arcane language. *Wherefore, thereby, aforesaid, hereinafter,* and *party of the first part* seldom appear in legal documents anymore, certainly not in sound legal writing. You tend to see less of the 50-word

294

sentence with multiple clauses and prepositional phrases, and more of the Hemingway style, simple and clear if not even blunt and impactful.

Precision is the important point. It may be hard to imagine, but contract claims and cases involving huge sums of money have turned on as a little as a single misplaced comma or equivalent grammar minutiae. One number, one word, one phrase, or one sentence can make all the difference, whether in drafting contracts, wills, trusts, powers of attorney, opinion letters, and other legal documents. Even in litigation, pleadings, court papers, jury verdict forms, and jury instructions must be clear, compelling, and precise. The spoken word is important to lawyers and their clients because of its command and eloquence, but the written word is critical to lawyers and their clients because of its consequences and effects. Legal writing is technical writing but often for a non-technical audience. If the parties do not understand their contracts, leases, mortgages, promissory notes, and buy-sell agreements, then it may hardly matter that their lawyers understand them.

Probably the main thing that makes lawyers better and better at writing, though, is not just the practice at it (many lawyers basically write all day, every day) but the practice under criticism. Lawyers often draft documents collaboratively within a law office. An associate writes the first draft, the partner corrects and amplifies it, and then another partner puts the finishing touches to it, informing each prior writer. Yet lawyers also often draft documents that their opposing counsel will critique and correct. Joint pretrial orders, stipulated orders, and consent judgments, for example, are joint documents that opposing lawyers must prepare and approve as to form, even if they and their clients may barely agree or even strenuously object to the content and meaning of those documents. Lawyers, in other words, must please one another and their clients when no one is ready for pleasing. Judges relatively often must settle disputed language between opposing lawyers.

Even when lawyers are writing their own documents alone, without collaboration or competing effort, they often do so with judges and opposing counsel taking issue with the form and content of their expressed thought. Briefing issues is a competition of the writers as much as of the writers' theories and minds. A well-written brief stands a chance on just about any argument. A poorly written brief stands a chance on few or none. Writing under constant surveillance and critique, and vigorous opposition, simply improves a writer. When you must defend and justify every written assertion, your writing craft improves.

So don't hesitate to ask a lawyer to document whatever it is that is important to you or your group. Lawyers usually get it right, or as nearly as one can, when it comes to writing.

4

Your Place or Mine?

Question

I was downtown the other day and noticed a bunch of law firms in the premier office tower that I was visiting. In fact, it looked like one law firm was taking up the top three floors. You lawyers must all have the fanciest digs. Where's your office?

Answer

Don't have one, although you wouldn't know it.

Actually, most lawyers do have offices, and many lawyers, especially those in large firms serving corporate clients, have very nice offices in the kind of you noticed on your downtown visit. To maintain and build their law practices, lawyers try to meet client expectations. For quite a while, many corporate clients retaining expert counsel have had high expectations for the kind of office they expect that counsel to maintain. Premier space in a premier building with a premier location can suggest premier service. Those client expectations are in large part the reason for those premier offices. Would you treat with a surgeon who worked out of a rundown location? Corporate legal matters can be just plain

297

important enough that corporations will pay the proverbial top dollar for legal representation to ensure its high quality.

Lately, though, global competition and other economic trends have encouraged corporations to look closely at their costs including the cost of law services. Corporate clients may be much more willing today than previously to retain lawyers in firms that are prudent about their own cost structures. After the salary and benefits of the lawyers in the firm, the firm's lease can be one of the next biggest expenses. A premier lease in a fancy office building can make the costs of the law firm's services significantly more expensive. Corporate clients may more often accept lower-cost suburban offices for their retained counsel, particularly if the firm has access to or maintains a smaller premier downtown space. Law firms are getting smarter about costs as clients get smarter about costs.

Individual, consumer, and small-business clients often do not have the same expectations around a law firm's offices as do corporate clients. When individual and small-business clients see their lawyer in a premier office, their first reaction may be that they cannot afford the lawyer's representation. Their expectation may be that the lawyer maintain a more-modest office, no matter the downtown or suburban location. While corporate-services firms occupy the premier office towers, consumer-services and small-business-services firms may occupy street-level storefront offices, offices in converted old homes near the courthouse, and offices in other convenient lower-cost spaces where individual and small-business clients feel most comfortable. Those lower-cost leases keep the firms' cost structure in line with their clients' ability to pay.

Many lawyers today find even lower costs, and are able to pass those savings on to their clients, by maintaining mobile offices. A lawyer may have no permanent office perhaps other than an office in the lawyer's home where the lawyer would not see clients. If the lawyer needs to meet with a client at a location other than the client's own office or home, then the lawyer may rent an office or conference room from another law firm or an office-suite provider, by the day or hour. The lawyer may have an of-counsel relationship with another law firm that permits the lawyer to borrow an office within the firm for a few minutes or couple hours in exchange for services that the lawyer provides the firm. The lawyer may then effectively work out of the lawyer's vehicle, carrying a smartphone, tablet, laptop computer, and portable printer where necessary. Lawyers find multiple arrangements for temporary

Some lawyers also maintain virtual offices. While clients once used a lawyer's office to certify that the lawyer had a legitimate presence within the professional community, today many clients use a lawyer's website, blog, social media, and other electronic presence to certify legitimacy. For some clients, a lawyer's physical office is not enough or at least means less than the lawyer's virtual presence. For some clients, a lawyer online may be more effective than a lawyer in an office offline. Lawyers with virtual practices may provide clients with remote video consultations and internet access to secure files and records to complete the virtual office. As clients' expectations change, lawyers change with them.

We live in a new digital and virtual world. Some law practices and services are peculiarly suited to that digital and virtual world. Expect to see continuing changes in the mobile and virtual practices of lawyers, although if you want a lawyer with a fancy office, then you can surely find one.

3

Clogging the Courts

Question

We must live in the most irresponsible society on earth. Everyone wants to blame someone else when something goes wrong. Why does everyone have to sue whenever someone looks sideways at them, clogging up the courts?

Answer

Actually, nuisance lawsuits, particularly personal-injury lawsuits of the kind you might have been assuming, really do not clog court dockets.

You read or hear about a few crazy verdicts in the news precisely because they are so anomalous. Yet when a runaway jury returns a verdict that the law and evidence does not support or that awards far more in damages than warranted, the trial judge has the power to reduce the damages or throw out the verdict. If the trial judge does not do so, then the appeals courts have the same power to correct verdicts. You seldom read or hear about these corrections, although they happen all the time.

Instead, you just read or hear about the initial result. Don't judge the justice system by the errors that it already corrects.

And by the way, any lawyer who files a frivolous lawsuit faces serious consequences. Those consequences include not only dismissal of the frivolous action but also monetary court sanctions against the lawyers and parties who file those actions. Those sanctions can include having to pay the other side's costs and attorney's fees for having to defend the frivolous action. Lawyers who file frivolous actions can also lose their license to practice law. Attorney discipline boards have the authority to reprimand lawyers privately or publicly. Licensing boards can also suspend a lawyer's license, requiring the lawyer to notify all clients, withdraw from all representation, and stop all legal work until the suspension ends. Licensing boards can also revoke a lawyer's license, effectively ending the lawyer's practice.

Filing frivolous cases would also be lousy business for lawyers, even if the courts and licensing boards were to let them get away with it. Personal-injury and other claims lawyers typically earn their fees on contingency from judgments and settlements. Their clients are often too poor to pay them anything up front, especially given how uncertain and expensive is claims litigation. Insurers settle with claimants only when their lawyers prove the merits of the cases that they file. While one can still find individual instances of nuisance lawsuits, they are generally not the problem creating clogged dockets.

On the other hand, some meritorious claims-type litigation can create docket-management problems. Asbestos litigation is an example. Asbestos and the lung diseases that it causes were a public-health disaster from which thousands died and many more suffered injury. The federal courts have consolidated asbestos cases so that they no longer clog courts across the country. Courts can also use class actions to manage extensive litigation whenever a defective product or careless practice causes such widespread harm that managing individual cases would be problematic.

301

So generally, claims-type litigation is not the problem. Americans have the privilege of effective law and functioning courts. That we all have ready access to the courts means a lot to the success of our society and economy. We are responsible individuals living in a law-based society. We permit and provide access to courts to adjust important rights while protecting litigants against frivolous actions.

That said, the courts have seen substantial increases in business lawsuits and family disputes, which have burdened some dockets. In any one local court, you may find that hospitals, banks, credit-card companies, and other businesses may file hundreds of actions to collect bad debt. Some family court judges and advocates call the situation within our families a crisis. Family courts deal not only with divorces but also paternity, support, custody, and separate-maintenance actions. Family, probate, and criminal courts also deal with abuse-and-neglect cases, guardianships, conservatorships, and adoptions. Most civil litigation involves these kinds of disputes, not personal-injury claims.

The point is that we need functioning courts where everyone, not just the rich and powerful, can find swift and affordable justice. Our justice system is far from perfect. Yet it may well be the best you can find anywhere in the world. Pay close attention to local issues about access to justice. We depend more on the courts than you probably imagined. You may just see, next time you need the courts.

2

Too Many Lawyers

Question

I see television ads, signs, and billboards for lawyers, and hear lawyers advertising on the radio. Do we really need all these lawyers? Aren't there too many lawyers?

Answer

Yes, we need the lawyers.

The nation has about 900,000 lawyers in private practice. That is about 1 lawyer for every 350 U.S. residents. The nation has many more accountants (about 1,760,000) than lawyers but somewhat fewer doctors (about 700,000). Only about two thirds of those who earn a law degree actually practice law. Other lawyers work in government, business, education, and the nonprofit sector.

Employment statistics suggest that we do not have too many lawyers. Only about two percent of lawyers are unemployed. The unemployment rate for all occupations is several times that number. Even during the depths of the latest recession, lawyer unemployment remained around two percent, while the rate for all occupations went to ten percent. Lawyers, doctors, and veterinarians traditionally have the lowest unemployment of the 50 or so professional occupations that the U.S. Bureau of Labor Statistics tracks. New lawyers take some time to pass the bar and find jobs and clients, but the nation does not have a large percentage of unemployed lawyers. The opposite is true that lawyers find plenty of good work to do.

Lawyers contribute to the nation's economy. Lawyers and their law firms give good paychecks to paralegals, administrative assistants, secretaries, bookkeepers, and other staff. Lawyers and their firms lease, buy, and build offices, which they fill with purchases of furniture, equipment, and even artwork. Lawyers and their firms buy supplies and services. Yet lawyers are also economic drivers for their clients. They help their corporate clients form companies, acquire capital, buy and sell goods and services, employ workforces, and protect inventions. They help their individual clients acquire, manage, control, and protect wealth, while passing it on to the next generation. Lawyers even help turn one unproductive household into two productive households, through divorce and other family law services.

In this economic context, asking if the nation has too many lawyers is like asking if it has too many butchers, bakers, and candlestick makers. In general, lawyers are marvelously productive, working famously long hours while juggling many matters. They use and manage their time, technology, transportation, and wits extraordinarily well, while helping others do so. Lawyers do not make tangible things like cars and furniture that you can readily see and appreciate, but they do make tangible documents like contracts and wills the effects of which are obviously beneficial. Lawyers are productive and valuable even when they are simply giving advice rather than drafting documents. For wayward clients, every course correction is a value add. While you often cannot see what lawyers produce, they are nonetheless hugely productive.

What you may have noticed is that lawyers advertise more today than they once did. Advertising is an important aspect of access. Not everyone has a lawyer on their block or in their congregation. Advertising is especially likely to reach and help those who do not know a lawyer, would have trouble locating one, would fear the cost, and would doubt themselves or their need or matter. Attorney discipline boards regulate lawyer advertising to ensure that it is accurate and not misleading, among other things. Lawyers who exaggerate their qualifications or results may lose their license.

Some people find lawyers offensive when they contact grieving individuals who have just suffered significant loss, say, after a car, plane, or train crash. Few of us would want a lawyer showing up at an accident scene or hospital, as film or television sometimes portray. Actually, though, conduct rules prohibit lawyers from in-person solicitation. You can call or visit a lawyer, but a lawyer should not be calling or visiting you seeking fee-based work without your invitation. Lawyers restrict their appeals to print and other advertising. States have also enacted rules prohibiting lawyers from any contact, even written appeals, within a reasonable period after an accident.

So if you have concerns over misleading or offensive advertising, contact your state's attorney discipline board or bar association for referral of the matter to investigators. We need the lawyers, but no lawyer should be giving all lawyers a bad name.

1

Representing the Guilty

Question

Did you see on the news last night what that murderer did to his victims? That is one thing that I will never understand about lawyers. How do lawyers justify representing the guilty?

Answer

Maybe none of us deserve lawyers, then.

We all break the law from time to time. For instance, very few of us stay within the speed limit all of the time. We get away with it most of the time, especially if we keep it to just five miles per hour over the limit. Yet we still break the law, even at five over. Of course, our lawlessness in one area does not make us lawless in other areas. Just because we routinely speed, or fail to come to a complete stop at stop signs, or run yellow-turning-red lights when we don't need to, or park illegally (but just for a few minutes!), doesn't make us murderers. We each break different laws in different ways with different degrees of reprehensibility.

Those differences highlight one reason that we need lawyers to represent us even when we are guilty. The role of a criminal-defense lawyer is not necessarily to set the guilty free. The role of

306

a criminal-defense lawyer is to ensure that the guilty get fair treatment. Crimes must fit the facts, and punishments must fit the crimes. If a police officer stopped you for speeding, then you would not want a ticket for running a red light. Criminal-defense lawyers ensure that those whom prosecutors charge with crime get charged only with the crime that they actually committed. If you got a ticket for speeding, then you would not want to lose your license over it. Defense lawyers ensure that penalties fit the crime.

As strange as it may seem, even homicide has its degrees. Imagine for a moment that a speeding driver just happens to strike and kill a child who unexpectedly darted out between parked vehicles. Or imagine for a moment that a mother takes her eyes off the road just long enough to check her crying child in the back seat but in doing so runs a red light, killing another motorist. Prosecutors may well charge both of those drivers with homicide. Should they receive the same charge and penalty as your murderer? Of course not. The appropriate charge might be something more like negligent vehicular operation causing death rather than first-degree murder. Yet it may well take a criminal-defense lawyer to ensure the right charge. Should those drivers spend a decade or two in prison alongside the murderer? Probably not, but again, a criminal-defense lawyer may be necessary to ensure the appropriate sentence.

Here, though, is where it may get hard for you. Even when it comes to the first-degree murderer, the criminal-justice system has its work to do. Not all murders are alike, just as not all murderers are alike. Moreover, not all whom juries convict of murder deserve the same sentence. Criminal-defense lawyers ensure that prosecutors, judges, and juries see those differences. The criminal-justice system is appropriately retributive. We punish because wrongdoers deserve punishment. Murderers ought to spend much time in prison. Yet the criminal-justice system is also appropriately redemptive. It rightly tries to bring the wrongdoer back into healthy and productive relationship with society. Don't we all often need forgiveness and redemption?

Some of the lawyers with the strongest morals, biggest hearts, and most-sensitive souls are criminal-defense lawyers. They take that role not to cheat the system and rob the victim. They take that role because they have unusual influence over the wrongdoer to help set the wrongdoer's life right. Those whom prosecutors charge with crime tend to listen to their criminal-defense lawyers. Criminals who never listened to anyone will listen to their lawyer when they face hard time. Criminal-defense lawyers will in the right instance beg their guilty clients to plead guilty under terms that redeem the criminal and repair the crime. Those lawyers will simultaneously negotiate with the prosecutor to fashion the sentence that will give the criminal the greatest reason and chance to reform from crime.

If you have doubts about the honesty of criminal-defense lawyers, then know that conduct rules bind them the same way that they bind prosecutors and other lawyers. Criminal-defense lawyers must not present witnesses whom they know to be lying. When a defense lawyer knows that his client committed the crime but the client intends to testify that the client did not, then that lawyer must disavow the testimony. Lawyers must not assist perjury. Other conduct rules prohibit lawyers from concealing evidence of crime or allowing clients to use their services to commit crimes. Lawyers who break these rules lose their law license.

If you still have a problem with criminal-defense lawyers, consider one last thing. When criminal-defense lawyers enforce their clients' constitutional rights to a fair trial, they are preserving the Constitution and criminal-justice system not just for the guilty but for all of us. Unfortunately, the criminal-justice system does convict the innocent, even if only relatively rarely. That wrongful convictions are reasonably rare testifies to the work of criminal-defense lawyers. That the wrongfully convicted sometimes find exoneration even after years of imprisonment testifies even more so to the work of criminal-defense lawyers.

Criminal-defense work may seem counter-intuitive, sometimes (involving the worst crimes) even immoral. In reality, it is usually anything but that. Be glad for criminal-defense lawyers, even as we should be glad for prosecutors.

Conclusion

So as the above examples show, people ask lawyers the darnedest questions. People have an innate curiosity about the law because they sense how important law is. They know intuitively that law has a lot to do with flourishing, meaning that those who follow law prosper while those who do not follow law starve. Yet people do not always understand law, indeed often misunderstand law. Many think that law is often nonsensical or counterintuitive when to the contrary it is rarely if ever so. Behind their questions are a slight distrust of law, when law must instead be trustworthy or it fails to work effectively as law and becomes something less than law. Law must have the confidence of the people. This book's purpose has been to make it so. Appreciate the law, but keep letting lawyers know your questions.

Author and Acknowledgments

Nelson Miller is professor and associate dean at Western Michigan University Thomas M. Cooley Law School, for which Dean Miller acknowledges gracious support of this practical scholarship. Dean Miller also acknowledges and thanks Western Michigan-Cooley student Mike O'Leary for the inspiration for this book and student Sarah Rae Miller for many of the questions. Before joining Western Michigan-Cooley, Dean Miller practiced civil litigation for 16 years in a small-firm setting, representing individuals, corporations, agencies, and public and private universities. He has published 22 books and dozens of book chapters and articles on law and law practice. The State Bar of Michigan recognized Dean Miller with the John W. Cummiskey Award for pro-bono service, and Harvard University Press included him in its book study *What the Best Law Teachers Do*. Dean Miller earned his law degree at the University of Michigan before joining Fajen and Miller, P.L.L.C., his practice base before beginning full-time law teaching. The author particularly thanks the students, full-time and adjunct faculty, and staff of the school's Grand Rapids, Michigan campus. An intimate local law school campus is a precious thing. Keep answering the important questions, my gracious friends.

Index

www.ingramcontent.com/pod-product-compliance
Lightning Source LLC
Chambersburg PA
CBHW060327220326
41598CB00023B/2627